P · O · C · K · E · T · S

CASTLES

D0784725

FALCONRY

15TH-
CENTURY
SPANISH PLATE

14TH-CENTURY
JOUSTER

WAR SWORD

P · O · C · K · E · T · S

CASTLES

Written by
PHILIP WILKINSON

LADY OF THE CASTLE

HEDINGHAM
CASTLE, ENGLAND

15TH-CENTURY "GOTHIC"
ARMOUR

DORLING KINDERSLEY
London • New York • Stuttgart • Moscow • Sydney

A DORLING KINDERSLEY BOOK

Project editor	Selina Wood
Designer	Janet Allis
Senior editor	Alastair Dougall
Senior art editors	Carole Oliver
	Sarah Crouch
Picture research	Victoria Walker
Production	Kate Oliver

First published in Great Britain in 1997
by Dorling Kindersley Limited
9 Henrietta Street, Covent Garden, London WC2E 8PS

Visit us on the World Wide Web at
http://www.dk.com

A CIP catalogue record for this book is available from
the British Library

ISBN 0 7513 5599 2

Colour reproduction by Colourscan, Singapore
Printed and bound in Italy by L.E.G.O.

CONTENTS

HOW TO USE THIS BOOK

These pages show you how to use *Pockets: Castles*. The book is divided into eight sections. The main sections consist of information about life in a castle and castles around the world. There is an introductory section on early castles at the front of the book and a reference section at the back, as well as a glossary and comprehensive index.

HEADING
The heading describes the overall subject of the page. This page is about castle lords. If a subject continues over several pages, the same heading applies.

CORNER CODING
The corners of the main section pages are colour coded.

- TYPES OF CASTLES
- CASTLE DWELLERS
- THE GARRISON
- DAILY LIFE
- ATTACK AND DEFENCE
- CASTLES AROUND THE WORLD

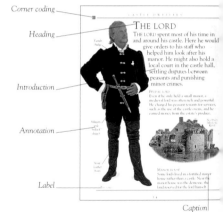

Corner coding

Heading

Introduction

Annotation

Label

CASTLE DWELLERS

THE LORD

THE LORD spent most of his time in and around his castle. Here he would give orders to his staff who helped him look after his manor. He might also hold a local court in the castle hall, settling disputes between peasants and punishing minor crimes.

FEUDAL LORD
Even if he only held a small manor, a medieval lord was often rich and powerful. He charged his peasant tenants for services, such as the use of the castle ovens, and he earned money from the estate's produce.

MANOR HOUSE
Some lords lived in a fortified manor house rather than a castle. Near the manor house was the demesne, the land reserved for the lord himself.

Caption

INTRODUCTION
The introduction provides an overview of the subject. After reading this, you should have a clear idea of what the pages are about.

CAPTIONS AND ANNOTATIONS
Each illustration has a caption. Annotations, in *italics*, point out features of an illustration and usually have leader lines.

RUNNING HEADS
These remind you which
section you are in. The
top of the left-hand page
gives the section name,
and the top of the right-
hand page gives the
subject heading.

FACT BOXES
Many pages have fact
boxes. These provide at-a-
glance information about
the subject, such as how
many arrows an archer
usually carried.

FEATURE BOXES
These boxes provide
additional information.
This book contains
a box giving details
on castle loopholes.

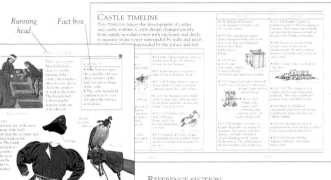

Running head

Fact box

REFERENCE SECTION
The reference section pages are tinted yellow and
appear at the back of the book. Here you will find
useful facts, figures, and charts. These pages
contain information on amazing castles, a timeline
of castle warfare, and a list of useful addresses.

LABELS
For clarity, some pictures
have labels. They may give
extra information or identify
a picture when it is not
obvious from the text
what it is.

INDEX
At the back of the book, there is an index.
It lists alphabetically every subject included
in the book. By referring to the index,
information on particular topics can
be found quickly and easily.

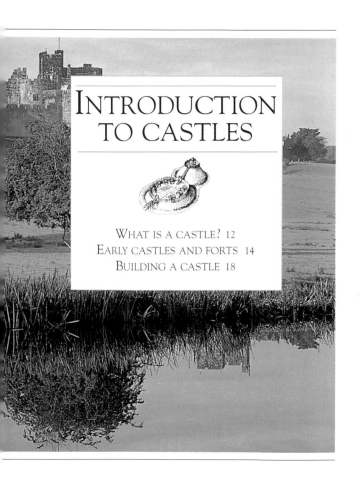

INTRODUCTION TO CASTLES

WHAT IS A CASTLE?

A CASTLE IS A DUAL-PURPOSE BUILDING – both a fortress and a residence. Most were built during the Middle Ages (*c*.1000–1500). A castle was home to a lord and his family, and he was responsible for providing men to fight for his king. The castle was a base for these men and a local stronghold where others could shelter in times of war. Because of their two roles, castles have many interesting features that tell us a great deal about medieval life.

THE FORTRESS
A castle had to keep an enemy out and yet allow those inside to see and shoot at any attacker. The first line of defence was usually a ditch or moat, followed by a strong wall, and the last refuge was a great tower.

Siege engine

Curtain wall

Mural tower

Attackers using battering ram

Gatehouse and drawbridge

Moat

CASTLE COMPLEX

THE GREAT HALL, CHATEAU DE CHILLON

THE RESIDENCE
The lord's residence consisted of a hall (a combination of living room, dining room, and office), and one or more private rooms where the lord and his family slept. Nearby was a kitchen complex, which might include a pantry, buttery, brewhouse, and bakehouse.

LORD OF THE LAND

Castles were built in an age when warfare was conducted by mounted warriors, or knights. A castle lord, who could be any noble from a king to a lesser baron, was a knight. In addition to his military role, he managed his estate and community.

Instead of signing documents, nobles added a wax seal. This seal die belonged to English knight, Robert FitzWalter.

13TH-CENTURY SEAL DIE

TYPICAL CASTLE?

Castle designs vary according to the site, the fashions of the time, and the taste of the lord. This big castle would have housed a large garrison. It shows most of the features seen in this book, but many castles were less elaborate.

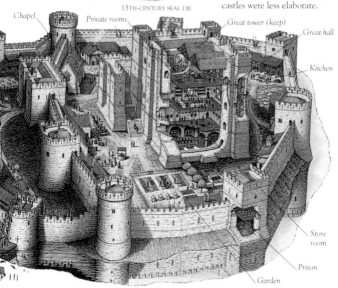

Chapel

Private rooms

Great tower (keep)

Great hall

Kitchen

Store room

Prison

Garden

EARLY CASTLES AND FORTS

TRUE CASTLES were first built in Europe in the Middle Ages. But many other, much earlier structures, are sometimes referred to as castles. These are usually either fortified settlements or forts built to house part of an army. They share some of the features of later castles, showing that medieval castle designers were part of a long line of fortification builders.

ORNAMENTAL STONE AT BOGAZKÖY

BOGAZKÖY, TURKEY
In the 13th century BC, the Hittites ruled an empire based in Turkey. Their capital, at Bogazköy, was protected by stone walls with square towers. As in later castles, the fortress gates were the most strongly fortified areas.

GATEHOUSE AT BOGAZKÖY

EARLY FORT FACTS

• The stones forming Mycenae's Lion Gate, each weigh around 20 tonnes (22 tons).

• Some Roman forts covered 24 hectares (60 acres) and could house more than 5,000 men.

BUHEN, EGYPT
The ancient Egyptians built the great fortress of Buhen to defend their southern borders. It had many additions made to it during the Egyptian New Kingdom (1550–1070 BC). The fortress was rectangular, with mud-brick walls, massive gatehouses, and square towers. Archers scanned the Nile river from the battlements.

FRONTIER FORTRESS AT BUHEN

MYCENAE, GREECE

From the 16th to the 12th centuries BC, much of mainland Greece was dominated by small, separate kingdoms, each with its own fortified citadel. The most famous of these citadels is at Mycenae. It is surrounded by walls built of huge stones. The walls protected many houses as well as a palace.

LION GATE AT MYCENAE CITADEL

IRON-AGE FORT

During the 1st century BC, Iron-Age hill-forts were built in Britain. They were protected by great earthworks (barriers made of earth) that must have taken years to create. At the top, a wooden palisade (fence) surrounded buildings.

MAIDEN CASTLE, ENGLAND

Settlement   Palisade

ROMAN FORT

The Roman legions built forts throughout Europe to a standard, rectangular plan. Some were built quickly from wood; others were more permanent structures of brick or stone.

ROMAN FORT c.120

More about early castles

In medieval Europe the first castles appeared in the 9th century, when the Carolingian empire was collapsing as a result of Viking and Magyar raids. As central authority disintegrated, nobles fought for power and territory. They built castles so that they could control and defend their land. Most castles were simple, wooden structures, relying on natural defences such as rivers or hills. Soon builders developed earthworks – mounds, banks, and ditches – for extra defence. Many castles were later rebuilt in stone, making use of the old earthworks.

Wooden tower

Motte

GERMAN MOTTE

MOTTES AND RINGWORKS
Earthworks could be mounds, called mottes, or round, raised enclosures, called ringworks. A motte housed a wooden tower; a ringwork contained buildings protected by a wooden palisade. Earth for both castle types was dug from the perimeter area, leaving a protective ditch.

STONE BUILDERS
Stone castle building began at the very start of the Middle Ages, and soon replaced timber castles. The earliest known stone tower was built at Doué-la-Fontaine, France, in c.950. Stone castles needed more workers, were more expensive, and took much longer to build than wooden ones, but were fireproof and more secure.

BUILDING A STONE TOWER

16

ADAPTING A MOTTE

Sometimes stone towers were built on the top of existing mottes. In the 12th century, Henry I built a shell keep (high circular wall with buildings around the inside) on William I's 11th-century motte at Windsor, England. Later, Henry II built a taller oval tower inside the shell.

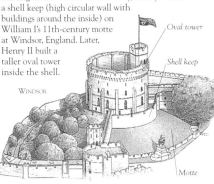

Oval tower

Shell keep

WINDSOR

Motte

RE-USING ROMAN FORTS

The Romans left behind many brick or stone forts, which were sometimes converted into castles in later centuries. At Portchester, England, a square Norman great tower, and other buildings, nestle in one corner of a large Roman fort.

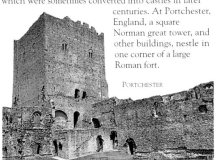

PORTCHESTER

DEFENDING A COUNTRY

Castles played a vital part in defence. An invading army had to take any castles in its path as it entered a country, a process that greatly slowed down the soldiers. If they ignored the castle, the garrisons could emerge and attack them from the rear. Otherwise, the garrisons of several castles could combine to make a formidable defensive army.

Defensive army launches counter-attack

Invading army attacks castles

BUILDING A CASTLE

MASTER MASON   CARPENTER

THE FIRST STEP in building a castle was to choose a good site – preferably one with its own water supply, and natural defences. The lord provided the materials, but the master mason organized the workforce. Labourers hauled heavy loads from wooden scaffolding and mixed up mortar. They built thick walls packed with stone rubble and flints.

THE WORKERS
A small army of men was needed to build a castle. They ranged from labourers to skilled workers, such as smiths, masons, and carpenters, with a master mason in charge.

BLACKSMITH

LUMP HAMMER

DIVIDERS
For intricate work, a mason drew a template or plan for each stone on parchment. He then used a pair of dividers to measure each dimension on the plan and transfer the measurement to the stone.

Pitching tool for making clean breaks in rough stone

HAMMERS AND CHISELS
Stone blocks were cut to size with a saw. The mason then trimmed them using a hammer and metal chisels. Large chisels were used for removing big chunks; smaller ones, for finer work.

HAMMER-HEADED CHISELS

"Punch" for chipping off large chunks of stone

DIVIDERS

SQUARE

THE SQUARE
A metal square, fashioned to 90 degrees, was used to square off corners of blocks of stone.

SINKING SQUARE
The mason used an adjustable, or "sinking", square to measure the depth of any holes he had to cut in the stone. This tool could also be used to check right-angles.

Oak stave   Wattle   Daub   Plaster

"Stock" rests on top of the stone

SINKING SQUARE

WATTLE AND DAUB
Courtyard buildings did not have to be as strong as the outer walls. Wooden frameworks were filled in with wattle (thin branches woven like basketwork) and daub (mud mixed with straw and manure), and covered with white plaster.

Blade measures depth

CONSTRUCTION SITE
In this 15th-century illustration, the lord and master mason are overseeing construction work. It could take 10 or even 20 years to complete a stone castle.

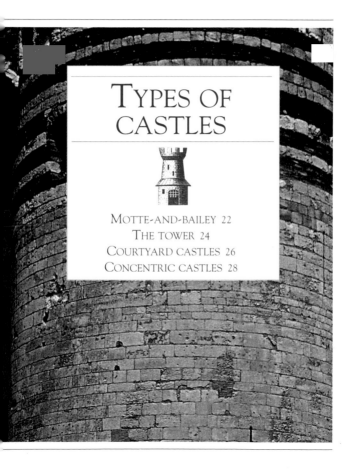

TYPES OF CASTLES

MOTTE-AND-BAILEY

MANY EARLY CASTLES consisted of an earth mound, or motte, topped with a wooden tower, and a courtyard, or bailey, which contained other buildings. Protected only by wooden fences and a ditch, these motte-and-bailey castles were vulnerable to attack by fire.

THE BAYEUX TAPESTRY

ANCIENT REMAINS
A ditch, motte, and earthworks around the bailey are all that remain of most motte-and-bailey castles. The flat-topped motte at Pleshey, England, is over 15 m (50 ft) tall.

BUILDING
Motte-and-baileys could be built in a matter of weeks. When William of Normandy invaded England in 1066, he constructed Hastings and Dover Castles within two weeks of landing (above).

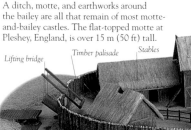

Lifting bridge

Timber palisade

Stables

Hall

Courtyard or bailey

Motte

Bailey

Motte

LEWES

This unusual English castle
with two mottes, was built in *c*.1169
by Gulielmus de Warenne, William I's
chief political officer. The mottes were
made with earth from the ditches,
and lumps of chalk. The wooden
buildings were later replaced by
stone structures.

Wooden tower
on stilts

Timber
walkway

MODEL OF MOTTE-
AND-BAILEY

Timber flying
bridge

MOTTE-AND-BAILEY
The motte's tower was a
refuge during war and,
in some cases, housed
the lord and his family.
The bailey often
contained a hall,
buildings for
livestock, a forge
and armoury,
and a chapel.

Earth mound
or motte

THE TOWER

THE FIRST STONE CASTLES were built in the 10th century and were usually centred on a large tower. The great stone tower, donjon, or keep was much stronger than its timber predecessor, and its height gave defending soldiers a good view and better line of fire.

HEDINGHAM
Built by the Norman lord, Aubrey de Vere in c.1140, this keep is made from a smooth stone called ashlar.

INSIDE A TOWER
A great tower provided a room for the garrison, and a hall where the lord took his meals. Above the hall was the lord and lady's bedroom. From the corner turrets guards could look out for the enemy.

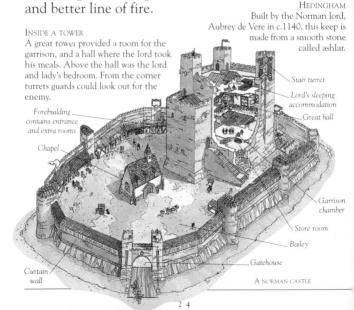

Stair turret

Lord's sleeping accommodation

Great hall

Forebuilding contains entrance and extra rooms

Chapel

Garrison chamber

Store room

Bailey

Gatehouse

Curtain wall

A NORMAN CASTLE

TOUR DE CESAR, PROVINS

OCTAGONAL TOWER
This eight-sided tower designed by French castle-builders, gave defending soldiers several lines of fire.

ROUND TOWER
Attackers could undermine a square tower by tunnelling under one corner so that it collapsed. Round towers, like this one at Pembroke, Wales, were more difficult to destroy.

PEMBROKE

BY THE FIRE
In a wooden hall, the fire had to be in the middle of the room, but stone towers contained fireplaces built in the wall and chimneys.

Zigzag ornamentation typical of 12th century

ROCHESTER

FIREPLACE

ROCHESTER
This huge tower, built in the 1120–30s is 38 m (125 ft) tall and has walls 3.7 m (12 ft) thick. Large windows were built on the upper floors to let in light. The windows lower down were little more then slits, to protect against enemy arrows.

COURTYARD CASTLES

SOME CASTLES CONSISTED OF
a courtyard protected by a
strong, stone curtain wall.
Along the wall were towers,
and usually a well-defended
gatehouse. A great tower was
not needed in this type of
castle because a hall and
other rooms were built
inside the courtyard, or
in the wall towers
or gatehouse.

CHATEAU
DE SAUMUR

Stair tower

Well house

COURTYARD WELL
At Saumur, France, a stair tower
gave access to all rooms in the
other towers and walls (above).
The well beneath the
courtyard was a vital
source of water
during a siege.

CHATEAU DE SAUMUR
This courtyard castle
stands on a stone
platform high above
the River Loire.
By the early
14th century,
it had large
towers with
luxurious rooms.

Defensive platform

Conical-roofed tower

Machicolations

CAERNARFON

English king Edward I built many castles in Wales during a campaign to invade and conquer the country. Some were designed as courtyard castles. At Caernarfon, the courtyard contained galleries at different heights, allowing defenders to fire from several levels.

CAERNARFON

BODIAM

This small English castle was built in the late 14th century by Sir Edward Dalyngrygge, a local lord, as part of a plan to defend England against a possible invasion from France. The castle was defended by an artificial lake that surrounded the whole building.

CONCENTRIC CASTLES

DURING THE 13TH CENTURY, lords began to build castles with two concentric rings (one inside the other) of defensive walls. The idea may have come from knights who had seen the twin walls of the city of Constantinople (Istanbul) during the crusades.

BEAUMARIS
Concentric castles had two advantages: firstly, attackers had to get through two barriers; secondly, defending archers could stand on both sets of walls, thus unleashing more fire power. Beaumaris in Wales was built between 1295 and 1330. It had two walls, as well as a moat.

Round-shaped tower gives many lines of fire

Inner walls are almost 5 m (16 ft) thick

BEAUMARIS

Low, outer wall with mural towers

CAERPHILLY

This castle was built by English nobleman Gilbert de Clare in the late 13th century, to defend his lands against the Welsh. Concentric walls and complex waterworks make this one of the best-defended of all castles.

Low, outer wall

High, inner tower

CAERPHILLY

Leaning tower

THROUGH THE WINDOW

Windows were usually high up in the walls. Even so, they had iron bars to keep out intruders.

Arrow-slits (loopholes) are narrow to protect archers behind them

GATEHOUSE, CAERPHILLY

GATEHOUSE

This outer gatehouse has arrow-slits for defending archers and once had a drawbridge, controlled by chains that passed through holes above the doorway. Attackers had to pass through two more gatehouses in order to storm the castle.

Broad moat

Barbican provides extra defence for southern gatehouse

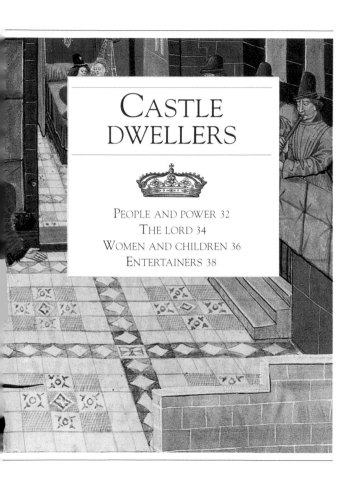

CASTLE DWELLERS

PEOPLE AND POWER

IN THE MIDDLE AGES, land was power. All the land belonged to the king, but he gave grants of land, called fiefs, to his nobles, who built castles to defend their land. In return for land and protection, the nobles had to swear allegiance to the king and provide him with soldiers during times of war.

THE KING

BISHOPS

Bishops were as powerful as nobles and frequently acted as advisers to the king. They often lived in castles and, like other nobles, could grow rich on the taxes, or tithes, that they collected from people who lived in their area.

BISHOP

THE KING

The king was at the top of the land-holding or "feudal" system. Keeping some land for himself, he built castles across his kingdom. When he visited them, his court accompanied him.

BARON

BARONS

The barons were the most powerful nobles. They held their fiefs directly from the king. In return for these large estates, each baron had to provide several thousand men to fight for the king. Otherwise, they had to pay a levy, known as a "shield money".

LORD

PEASANT

LESSER LORDS

Lesser lords, or knights, held fiefs from the barons in return for military service. Unlike the barons' vast fiefs, a lord's estate could be small – often only a village, with its castle or fortified manor house.

PEASANTS

Medieval peasants were allotted small areas of land by their local lord, which they could farm. They had to give some of the produce to the lord, who owned everything they used.

THE LORD

THE LORD spent most of his time in and around his castle. Here he would give orders to his staff who helped him look after his manor. He might also hold a local court in the castle hall, settling disputes between peasants and punishing minor crimes.

Family badge

Military-style "bollock" dagger

Stout, leather boots

THE LORD

FEUDAL LORD
Even if he only held a small manor, a medieval lord was often rich and powerful. He charged his peasant tenants for services, such as the use of the castle ovens, and he earned money from the estate's produce.

SCOTNEY MANOR, KENT

MANOR HOUSE
Some lords lived in a fortified manor house rather than a castle. Near the manor house was the demesne, the land reserved for the lord himself.

LORD AND BAILIFF

THE LORD'S DUTIES
Most lords kept a close eye on the running of the estates, meeting key officials every day to check the progress of work in the fields. This French lord is discussing his demesne with one of his officials.

OFFICIALS
The steward, one of the most important of the lord's officials, kept the accounts and organized work on the manor. The bailiff allocated jobs to the peasants, and the reeve oversaw the peasants as they worked.

Hood to keep bird calm

FALCONRY

Felt hat

Woollen, linen-lined jacket with pewter buttons

BAILIFF'S CLOTHES

RECREATION
As well as hunting with hounds, many lords enjoyed falconry – training birds of prey to catch small game. Powerful birds were very valuable; eagles were reserved for kings to fly, while ladies flew small birds such as merlins.

WOMEN AND CHILDREN

MOST MEDIEVAL WOMEN spent their lives at home, looking after the house and children. They did everything from spinning and weaving to keeping accounts. Even so, anything a woman owned became her husband's when she married.

Jewelled head-dress

THE LADY
The wife of a knight supervised the kitchens, kept the household accounts, brought up the children, and entertained guests. She also helped to run the estate when her husband was away on business or at war.

Decorated hairpins

"Horned" head-dress

NOBLE FASHIONS
Most women wore woollen or linen clothes, but noblewomen dressed more fashionably. Fur-trimmed gowns and elaborate head-dresses were popular in the 14th century.

MEDIEVAL FEMINIST

Few women could read and write in the Middle Ages, but Christine de Pisan (1364–1430), made her living from writing. She wrote love poems, books on history, philosophy, and the defence of women (right).

Box hat

Woollen doublet

A boy became a page around the age of seven

Leather sandals

THE PAGE
A page was a well-born boy who was sent to live in a great lord's household to learn about life at court, including the art of courtly manners and how to serve a knight.

PLAYING THE KNIGHT
Boys of noble birth liked to play at being knights. A rich father had miniature swords and armour made for his sons; poorer boys used wooden swords.

BOY'S BACKPLATE

BOY'S BREASTPLATE

SMALL SWORD

ENTERTAINERS

Minstrel

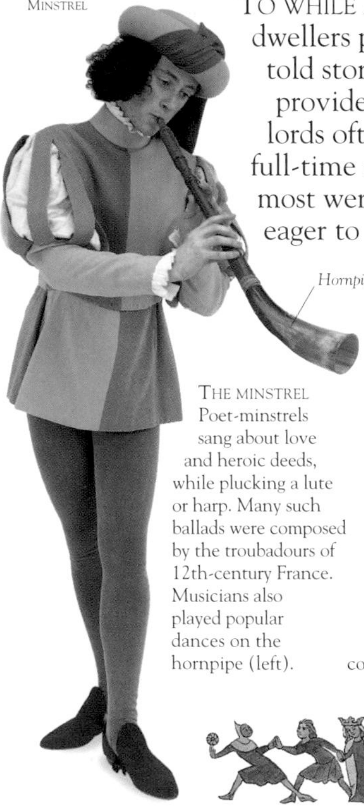

TO WHILE AWAY the evenings, castle
dwellers played games, sang songs,
told stories, or listened to music
provided by minstrels. Rich
lords often employed their own
full-time minstrels and jesters, but
most were travelling entertainers,
eager to "sing for their supper".

Hornpipe

THE MINSTREL
Poet-minstrels
sang about love
and heroic deeds,
while plucking a lute
or harp. Many such
ballads were composed
by the troubadours of
12th-century France.
Musicians also
played popular
dances on the
hornpipe (left).

ONE-MAN BAND
To accompany a dance, a musician
would play a pipe with his left hand
while beating a
drum called a
tabor with
his right.

Tabor

Pipe

CHAIN DANCE
In a common 12th-century dance, the
company weave in and out along a line or
circle, in time to the music.

PIPES

Bagpipes were popular worldwide. The most common bagpipe had a pipe called a chanter, which was used to play the melody, and one or more drones that played a continuous note under the melody.

Drone produces single, continuous note

Bag

Mouthpiece

Chanter, used to play a range of notes

BAGPIPES

ORGANISTRUM

COURT JESTER

The job of the jester (or fool) was to make nobles laugh. He might wear bells and carry a bladder on a stick (a slapstick), and his jokes could be very crude.

COURT JESTER

ORGANISTRUM

This instrument was used in southern Europe, in the 11th century. One player turned the handle, while another operated keys to play the strings.

CANTERBURY TALES

STORYTELLING

Kings or lords employed poets to tell them stories. Those who could not afford this luxury told stories to each other. Geoffrey Chaucer's *The Canterbury Tales* is a famous medieval poem about a group of pilgrims who tell each other stories to pass the time on their way to Canterbury.

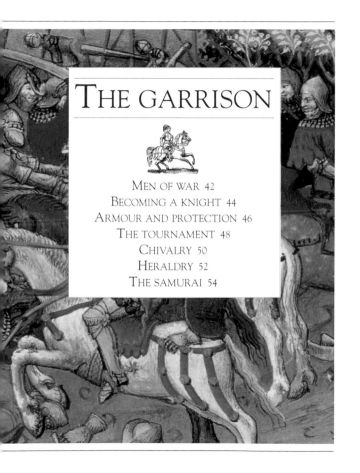

THE GARRISON

MEN OF WAR

THE BODY of soldiers who lived in a castle and
defended it was called the garrison. In early
castles, especially in times of war, knights
lived permanently in their lord's castle.
Later, more knights had their own estates
and they would spend only short periods at
their lord's castle.

Wheel pommel
with cap

POINTED SWORD
In the 14th century,
pointed swords were
made. They were used for
stabbing between the gaps in
an opponent's plate armour.

THE SWORD
The knight's main weapon
was his sword, which could be
wielded with one hand while
he was on horseback. This
double-edged weapon (left)
was used to slash and cut
down the enemy.

Two-handed
sword

Battle axe

FORWARD INTO BATTLE
The garrison provided a
ready supply of warriors to
defend the castle and
lord, and to go to war.
This 15th-century
battle scene shows
knights charging at
each other with swords,
battle axes, and lances.

15TH-CENTURY FRENCH BATTLE SCENE

FIGHTING ON FOOT

The garrison included foot soldiers who fought alongside knights. They preferred staff weapons – axes, hammers, and blades mounted on poles – and a sword and buckler shield for close combat.

Small fist-shield, or buckler, for punching

"BOLLOCK" DAGGER

Single-handed sword for hand-to-hand combat

HAND-TO-HAND WEAPONS

DAGGERS

From lord to humblest soldier, most men carried a dagger. The handle was shaped to stop the hand from slipping onto the blade.

GLAIVE

This was one of the staff weapons used by medieval foot soldiers. Its pointed blade was ideal for stabbing.

GLAIVE

SOLDIERS

Most ordinary soldiers could afford only a few pieces of armour – to which they added any plates they picked up on the battlefield. A 15th-century soldier wore a quilted "jack" over his "arming" doublet, a simple helmet, and plate armour to protect his hands and arms.

"Sallet" helmet

WAR HAMMER

This hammer with a sharp point could pierce plate armour. It could also concuss an opponent.

Mitten gauntlet

WAR HAMMER

Close-fitting canvas "arming" doublet

BECOMING A KNIGHT

CERTAIN NOBLE YOUTHS aged about
14 became squires, or knight's
apprentices. The squire had to look
after the knight's horses and armour,
and come to his master's aid in
battle. He also learned warfare and
horsemanship. The training was
hard – not all squires succeeded
in becoming knights.

DUBBING

Successful squires were
knighted at around the age
of 21, by another knight or
the king, in a special ceremony.
Before the 13th century, new
knights were tapped on the head
with a sword; later, on each shoulder.

TRAINING

Squires took part in sports such as wrestling, throwing
javelins, stone-putting, and acrobatics. They also
fought with staffs or swords. These activities kept the
young men fit and helped prepare them for battle.

TRAINING FOR BATTLE

THE SQUIRE

As well as acquiring military
skills, the squire had to serve
his lord at table. He was
taught to be brave, to protect
the weak, and respect women.

44

ARMING A KNIGHT
One of the squire's most important duties was to help a knight put on his armour. First, the knight donned an "arming" doublet. This was a padded jacket with panels of mail under the arms and leather thongs with which to fasten armour pieces.

"Arming" doublet

Helmet

FULLY ARMED KNIGHT

CHAIN MAIL
After the leg armour was fitted, a mail skirt was put on to protect the knight's lower stomach and groin – areas not covered by plate armour.

Elbow piece attached by laces

Leather glove inside gauntlet

DRESSED FOR BATTLE
The squire helped his master put on the various sections of plate armour, which finally covered the knight from head to toe. It took a long time to put on, but was jointed to allow the knight to move quite freely.

ARMOUR AND PROTECTION

THE FIRST KNIGHTS wore shirts made of mail to protect the upper body. Soon leggings of mail were added. In the 14th century, armour made up of solid metal plates became fashionable and gradually replaced mail. By the 17th century, the increasing efficiency of firearms was making armour obsolete.

BASINET

Viewing slit

Ventilation holes

BASINET
This typical helmet of late 14th-century Italy gives good protection from arrows and sword blows. Holes in the visor allow the knight to see and breathe. When the pin is removed, the visor swings away to one side.

Mail neck guard

KNIGHT'S EFFIGY
This effigy of *c.*1340 shows a knight wearing a coat of mail as a symbol of status.

MAIL SHIRT
Mail was made up of tiny iron rings joined together with rivets (see below). Mail was flexible, but it was heavy – a full coat could weigh up to 14 kg (31 lb) – and it did not protect against blows from maces and axes.

GAUNTLETS

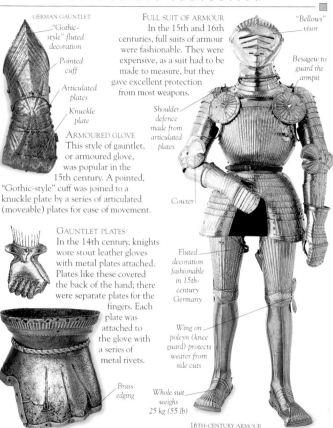

GERMAN GAUNTLET

"Gothic-style" fluted decoration

Pointed cuff

Articulated plates

Knuckle plate

FULL SUIT OF ARMOUR
In the 15th and 16th centuries, full suits of armour were fashionable. They were expensive, as a suit had to be made to measure, but they gave excellent protection from most weapons.

"Bellows" visor

Besagew to guard the armpit

Shoulder defence made from articulated plates

ARMOURED GLOVE
This style of gauntlet, or armoured glove, was popular in the 15th century. A pointed, "Gothic-style" cuff was joined to a knuckle plate by a series of articulated (moveable) plates for ease of movement.

Cowter

GAUNTLET PLATES
In the 14th century, knights wore stout leather gloves with metal plates attached. Plates like these covered the back of the hand; there were separate plates for the fingers. Each plate was attached to the glove with a series of metal rivets.

Fluted decoration fashionable in 15th-century Germany

Wing on poleyn (knee guard) protects wearer from side cuts

Brass edging

Whole suit weighs 25 kg (55 lb)

16TH-CENTURY ARMOUR

THE TOURNAMENT

TOURNAMENTS began as practice sessions for battle, but became popular courtly entertainment. Different types of combat were involved, including mock battles, jousts, and single combats; knights were sometimes killed in the fighting. Winners often won their opponents' horses and armour.

Solid hammer head

POLLAXE

Javelins, swords, and axes were popular in foot combat. The pollaxe was used to hit an opponent on the head and could concuss a man in armour.

Blunted wooden lance

FOOT COMBAT

In foot combat with swords, each knight was only allowed a fixed number of blows. If a knight broke the rules, or if the fight got out of hand, armed guards would intervene.

RECONSTRUCTION OF AN EARLY 14TH-CENTURY JOUST

Caparison, or colourful, decorated horse covering

THE TOURNEY
In a tourney, two teams of mounted knights fought a mock battle. Many knights suffered serious injuries. Hundreds – even thousands – of knights could take part, charging at each other with lances.

TILTING HELMET
When a jousting knight charged, he lowered his head, so that he could see through his helmet's eye slit. When he raised his head, his eyes were protected by the helmet's lip.

Eye-slit

FROG-MOUTHED HELMET

LANCER'S SHIELD
In some jousts, knights carried shields with curved edges to support their lances, like this one made in 15th-century Germany.

Curved edge to support lance

15TH-CENTURY SHIELD

Metal helmet

Shield painted in heraldic colours

THE JOUST
In a joust, mounted knights fought one against one. The object was to unhorse your rival with one blow of the lance. To make jousts safer, lances with blunt ends were often used.

CHIVALRY

KNIGHTS were expected to behave correctly at all times, although many knights failed to live up to this ideal. During the Middle Ages a special code of conduct, the code of chivalry, developed. It combined military virtues with those of Christianity, calling for respect for enemies, and for the weak.

CODE OF CONDUCT
The knight in Geoffrey Chaucer's *The Canterbury Tales*, is courteous and merciful. He follows the courtly code conscientiously and is highly respected by his fellow pilgrims.

MYTHS AND LEGENDS
Chivalry was epitomized in heroic legends, such as the *Chansons de Geste* of medieval France and *Le Morte d'Arthur* in England.

King Arthur's knights go on a quest for a lost religious relic, the Holy Grail. Only the most worthy knight, Sir Galahad, is granted a glimpse of it before he dies.

SIR GALAHAD

COURTLY LOVE
Medieval French writers developed the principles of courtly love. According to its rules, which existed more in literature than in real life, a knight vowed to be faithful to his lady.

Crusaders

Chivalric ideals
influenced the founding
of Christian military
orders during the
Crusades. These were holy
wars that took place from
1095 to 1291, to take
control of the "Holy
Land" of Palestine from
the Muslim Saracens.

CAPTURE OF JERUSALEM
The first crusaders arrived in
Jerusalem in 1099. They captured
and pillaged the city, founded several
small states in the area, but failed to
keep control of the city. Despite this
disaster, many crusader knights stayed
on in Syria and Palestine. They built
castles and grew rich robbing Muslim
pilgrims and traders.

Hospitaller knight

Templar knight

MILITARY ORDERS
Among the knights
who settled in the
Holy Land were orders
of "fighting monks", who
took religious vows but also
fought. They included the
Knights Templar, who
had their base near the
Temple in Jerusalem,
and the Hospitallers, who
specialized in healing the sick.

HERALDRY

IN THE TUMULT of a battle or tournament it was difficult work out who was who. So a system of symbols, called heraldry, was devised to make the identification of knights easier. Each noble was given a coat of arms, a symbol that only he and his men were allowed to wear.

HERALDIC LANGUAGE
The coat of arms consisted of a shield, a crest, and a pair of "supporters" – figures or animals placed on either side of the shield. They were designed by heralds, using colours and patterns to represent furs, such as ermine, and metals, such as gold. The designs are described in a language based on Old French.

Shield

The symbol, or "charge", is a dragon, sitting "sejant" (erect)

The surface, or "field" of the shield is gold

OR A DRAGON
SEJANT VERT

HERALDIC COLOURS	
OR	= GOLD
ARGENT	= SILVER
GULES	= RED
AZURE	= BLUE
SABLE	= BLACK
VERT	= GREEN
PURPURE	= PURPLE

AZURE A FLEUR
DE LYS (LILY) OR

ARGENT A MULLET
(STAR) AZURE

SYMBOLISM
Sometimes heralds designed visual clues. This plate bears a shield based on the arms of two Spanish kingdoms. Castile is represented by a castle and León, by a lion. The combination of arms indicates the marriage of two families.

BADGE OF OFFICE
Servants or men-at-arms often wore a badge bearing their lord's coat of arms. This 16th-century arm badge was worn by a servant of François de Lorraine, leader of the Knights Hospitaller in France.

Flag within a heraldic crest is quite unusual

FAMILY CREST
The crest is a symbol that was originally placed on top of a knight's helmet. It appears above the shield in a full coat of arms. This is the crest of the Churchill family. It shows a lion sejant (seated erect), with one paw raised, holding a flag.

OR A CHIEF
(HORIZONTAL SEGMENT)
INDENTED PURPURE

ERMINE (FUR) A
CROSS CROSSLET
GULES

GYRONNY
(TRIANGLES)
ARGENT AND GULES

VAIR (FUR) A
CHEVRON SABLE

IDENTIFICATION
A knight's coat of arms could appear on his shield, or on a surcoat worn over his armour or on his horse. At a tournament, bright colours and elaborate armour were also important for identification.

Horse's heraldic covering, called a caparison

THE TOURNAMENT

THE SAMURAI

THE WARRIORS of medieval Japan were called samurai. In a similar way to European knights, the samurai served a lord, rode a horse, wore armour, and lived in a castle. They wielded great power over local peasants, who grew food for the samurai.

SAMURAI KNIGHT ON HORSEBACK

MOUNTED WARRIOR
Until about 1300, the samurai fought mainly on horseback. Their principal weapons were bows and arrows, which they used against a distant enemy. Swords were used for close combat.

WAKIZASHI
A samurai warrior carried two swords sheathed in wooden scabbards. The shorter one, the *wakizashi*, was used in combat and for ritual suicide.

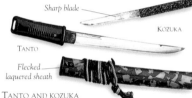

Sharp blade

KOZUKA

TANTO

Flecked laquered sheath

TANTO AND KOZUKA
A samurai had two knives, which he carried together in the same sheath – a dagger known as a *tanto*, and a small knife, called a *kozuka*. They had razor-sharp blades made of iron and steel.

WAKIZASHI

Wooden scabbard (saya)

EARLY ARMOUR

MODERN ARMOUR

O-YOROI ARMOUR
Armour of the *O-yoroi*
style was worn by
samurai in the 12th
and 13th centuries.
It was made of small
iron plates decorated
with laquer.

*Silk-laced
sleeves*

*The helmet
has a face
defence
(mempo)*

TOSEI GUSOKU
With the
appearance of
firearms during the
16th century,
Japanese armourers
strengthened their
armour with tougher
iron plates. They also
introduced the *tosei
gosoku* style, which
included guards for
the arms and legs.

*Samurai who wore this
armour were mounted
archers*

KATANA
The long samurai sword was called a
katana. The hilt was covered in shark
skin and bound with braid. This gave
a rough surface that would not easily
slip from the hand.

*Shark-skin
grip*

KATANA

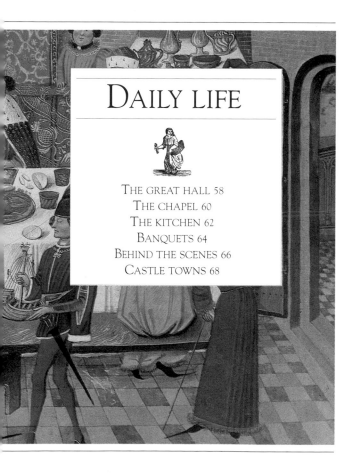

DAILY LIFE

THE GREAT HALL

THE HALL was the nerve centre of the castle. Here, meals were taken, guests were received, and castle business was carried out; it was also used as sleeping quarters. The castle's largest room, it was situated on one floor of the great tower, or on its own block in the castle courtyard. It was furnished with long trestle tables that could be taken down at night. Around these were benches and a chair for the lord.

ROYAL HALL
Loches Castle, France, has a 15th-century hall used by French king Charles VII. Its striking, stepped roof is flanked by round turrets giving a good view of the surrounding country.

ROYAL HALL, CHATEAU DE LOCHES

BANNERS
Knights carried banners into battle. They often bore the knight's coat of arms. When they were not in use they were hung up in the great hall for decoration.

HALL INTERIOR

The great hall at Hedingham Castle, England, takes up one floor of the great tower. Because it is on an upper floor, it has large windows. These, and the big fireplace make the room seem more comfortable than most great halls.

LEGAL BUSINESS

The lord's court, held in the hall, was used for resolving local disputes. Although most lords had no legal training, they had plenty of experience of dealing with people.

FLOOR COVERINGS

Carpets were unusual in the Middle Ages. Halls on ground floors had bare floors of stone or ceramic tiles; those on upper stories had wooden floors.

FLOOR TILE

TAPESTRY AT CHATEAU D'ANGERS

TAPESTRIES

A hall's stone walls were sometimes decorated with tapestries. These made the room more colourful, and could cut out draughts. This 14th-century example is from a series at Angers, France.

THE CHAPEL

IN THE MIDDLE AGES, everyone was expected to go to church on Sunday, so castles usually had a chapel. It could be built high in the great tower, above the gatehouse, or in its own separate building. Chapels were usually decorated with carvings, wall paintings, and sometimes stained-glass windows depicting Bible scenes.

A ciborium held consecrated bread for mass

Scene of the adoration of the Magi

Carvings of mythical beasts

MASS
Mass was held regularly by the castle chaplain. He was often the most educated resident, who helped the lord write his letters.

DECORATION
Biblical scenes and mythical beasts adorn this chapel doorway at Loches Castle, France. Few people could read, so looking at carvings was an important part of education.

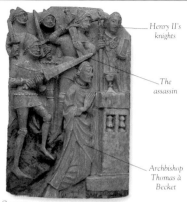

Henry II's
knights

The
assassin

Archbishop
Thomas à
Becket

SANCTUARY
A church or chapel was a place of sanctuary, where
anyone, even a criminal, could escape the clutches
of the law. In 1170, knights of Henry II of England
broke the law of sanctuary, when they murdered
Archbishop Thomas à Becket in Canterbury
cathedral, after he had argued with the king.

ST JOHN'S CHAPEL
The chapel at the Tower of
London is in the White Tower.
Its rounded arches, cylindrical
columns, and plain barrel-
vaulted ceiling are typical
Norman style of c.1090.

BURIAL
The chapel was where the lord and his family
were buried when they died. Some medieval
nobles were commemorated with large tombs
bearing life-size sculptures of the deceased. This
is the tomb of a 13th-century English knight.

COLOURFUL FLOORS
Chapel walls and floors were
sometimes covered with
ceramic tiles. These usually
bore abstract patterns, coats
of arms, or Bible stories.

THE KITCHEN

IN EARLY, wooden castles, the kitchen was usually in a detached building in the courtyard, to reduce the risk of fire. In stone castles, the kitchen was often placed near the hall, separated by a narrow passage. The room contained a large fire for cooking, tables for preparing food, and ovens for baking bread. Large castles had a separate bakery and brewhouse.

KITCHEN FIREPLACE AT PFALZGRAFENSTEIN, GERMANY

BOILING
The kitchen could have several fireplaces for cooking. A small fire was used for boiling food in an iron pot. The pot was hung from a metal chain, and the heat could be adjusted by moving the hook to vary the length of the chain.

ROASTING
A popular way of cooking meat was to roast a whole carcass on a spit over a fire. Several spit-roasted animals provided enough meat for a banquet. The spit was turned by hand; it was hot, dangerous work.

Cook puts log on fire using fork

Whole carcass is roasted on the spit

COOKING A ROAST

APPLE CORER

Hollow tube removes apple core

KNIFE

FLESH-HOOK

COOKING UTENSILS

In a manor or castle, head cooks were always men. They roasted, boiled, and baked vast quantities of food using large utensils such as flesh-hooks. A small army of boys, called scullions, washed up.

SEASONING

Herbs and spices were widely used in the Middle Ages to flavour food that could otherwise taste bland. They were also used to disguise the flavour of meat that was past its best!

Mint Sage Rosemary Parsley

Frame for hanging utensils

Adjustable ratchet

Small pot hanger

Large pot-hook for huge cauldron

Pot hook suspended from adjustable pot hanger

THREE-LEGGED POT

As an alternative to hanging a pot from a hook or chain, pots with legs were made to stand in the fire. Handles were added to help remove the pot from the fire.

POT HOOKS

Twin iron hooks were attached to the handles of a cauldron so that it could be hung over a fire. Several pots could be hung over a large castle fireplace.

BANQUETS

THE MAIN MEAL of the day, whether a simple dinner or an elaborate banquet, was served in the evening, in the castle hall. The grandest banquets lasted for hours. People ate vast amounts – there were several meat and fish courses, followed by various puddings.

15TH-CENTURY ILLUSTRATION

SERVING AT THE TABLE
Pages and squires often served the lord and his guests at table (left). It was common for singers and acrobats to entertain the diners between courses.

HIGH TABLE
The lord and guests sat at the high table, situated on a raised platform, or dais. The lord was the first to be served, after the food had been checked for poison by a servant taster.

Lord's seat at the centre of the table

Expensive wine glass

Rabbits, or coneys, were a common source of meat

Pigeons were baked in hot ashes

Geese were eaten on special occasions

GAME
Everything from rabbits to small birds like pigeons and finches was eaten at the low table. The lord and lady were more likely to enjoy swan or fattened goose.

LOW TABLE
Servants and other household members sat at low trestle tables set at right-angles to the high table, along the length of the hall. Food on these tables was less rich than that on the high table.

Large jug for ale

Large wooden platter

Spoons were placed face down to "keep the devil out"

Decorated ceramic jug

BREAD PLATES
Food was eaten off large pieces of dry bread called trenchers. The sauce seeped into the bread, which could be eaten at the end of the course, or thrown to the dogs.

PLACE SETTINGS
At high table, diners might eat off a pewter base and a wooden bowl. People used their own knives, which they carried around with them.

Wooden bowl for pottage

Drinking vessel

BEHIND THE SCENES

A MEDIEVAL CASTLE was a hive of activity. As well as men-at-arms preparing for battle, there might be builders at work, officials meeting the lord on business, and visitors from outlying estates. Many castles also echoed to the sounds of the farmyard, for animals were often kept to ensure a regular supply of food.

LONGHORN

PIG

BAGOT GOAT

ANIMALS
Some animals were kept in the courtyard; others were brought in from the fields at night. Farmers made use of the whole animal, tanning the hide to make leather, and using the horns for containers.

CARPENTER

Wool twists into yarn

SPINNING
Medieval clothes were made at home. Using a simple wooden spindle, women spun sheeps' wool into yarn, which could then be woven into cloth.

CASTLE MAINTENANCE
Damage caused during sieges or by wear and tear meant that castles had to be constantly repaired. Masons were on hand to mend stonework, and woodworkers to make doors, roofs, hoardings, and timber-framed buildings for the courtyard.

Broad axe

Private chambers

Most people slept in the place where they worked – the cooks in the kitchen, the armourer in his workshop, servants in the hall. But the lord and his family had their own rooms in a well-defended part of the castle, such as the great tower, gatehouse, or a strong wall tower.

Urinal: urine was saved and used for cloth finishing and dying

ON THE THRONE
Lavatories were very basic. Most castles had *garderobes* – lavatories connected to a stone chute that emptied into a moat or cesspit.

TOOTH POWDER

CUTTLE-FISH

WHELK

HYGIENE
Wealthy people used ground-up cuttlefish and shells to make a coarse powder for cleaning teeth. Soap could be made from animal fat and wood ash.

SLEEPING ARRANGEMENTS
The lord and lady slept in a wooden-framed bed, with woollen curtains to keep out draughts. There might also be a "truckle" bed on wheels underneath, for children or for servants (below).

CASTLE TOWNS

MANY MEDIEVAL TOWNS were surrounded by walls, and a castle sometimes formed part of the fortifications. It might be the home of the local lord or an official, such as a sheriff, who held the castle on behalf of the king. A sheriff kept order in the town and surrounding area. His castle was a combination of barracks, local government headquarters, residence, and prison.

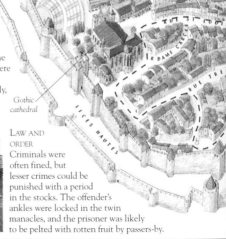

CARCASSONNE
This town in southern France still has its medieval walls, with the castle adjoining them on one side. The walls and castle were built in the 12th and 13th centuries by the ruling family, the Trencavels.

Gothic cathedral

THE STOCKS

LAW AND ORDER
Criminals were often fined, but lesser crimes could be punished with a period in the stocks. The offender's ankles were locked in the twin manacles, and the prisoner was likely to be pelted with rotten fruit by passers-by.

MARKET DAY

The right to hold a market was granted to a town by the king, in a document called a charter. A market was held once a week in the main street or central square. Traders and craftsmen set up stalls, and people came from the surrounding countryside to sell animals and produce. A market could bring great wealth to the community.

TOWN SCENE

Chateau Comtal

Gallo-Roman walls

The Great Well

Space used for crossbow practice

NIGHT WATCH

At sunset, medieval town bells rang to sound the curfew, when everyone had to be indoors. Nightwatchmen with lanterns patrolled the dark streets to deter criminals.

MEDIEVAL LANTERN

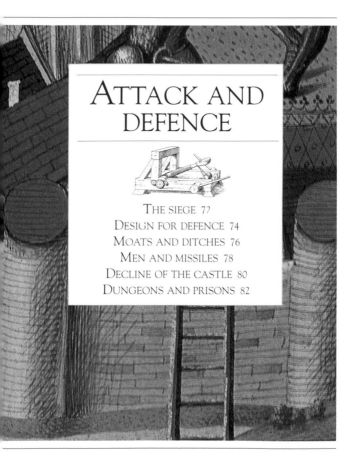

ATTACK AND DEFENCE

THE SIEGE

WHEN AN ARMY attacked a castle, it surrounded the walls so that no one could get out. Battering rams and other large weapons called siege engines were used to break into the castle. Usually, the inhabitants ran out of food and surrendered before a castle was stormed.

Sling

Garrison defends the castle with fire

TREBUCHET

The trebuchet was a large wooden catapult used to hurl large stones at castle walls. It was first used in the 12th century. Several men yanked on the ropes to swing the other end of the wooden arm upwards, letting loose a boulder from the sling.

Pivoting arm

Ropes for hauling

TRACTION TREBUCHET

MINING

Under cover of a wooden shelter on wheels, attackers could dig out the foundations of a castle to make it collapse. Wooden siege towers were also wheeled next to castle walls, so attackers could storm the castle.

BALLISTA

Like a giant crossbow, a ballista shot a huge metal bolt. It was not as easy to aim as a hand-held crossbow, but could be kept pointed at the gatehouse, in case the defenders tried to escape.

Rachet for keeping tension on skeins

Winch

Bow cord

BALLISTA

SIEGE FACTS

• In 1204, soldiers attacking Chateau-Gaillard in France got in by climbing up the lavatory shaft.

• Sometimes the easiest way to get into a castle was to bribe the guards.

• Castles were built with secret tunnels for smuggling in supplies during a siege.

Rope to winch arm down

Wooden cup for missile

Skein of twisted ropes provides power

FRONT VIEW OF CATAPULT

MANGONEL

Twisted ropes provided the power for the mangonel, a type of catapult copied from the Romans. Sometimes dead animals or the heads of captured soldiers were fired over castle walls to upset the defenders.

SCALING THE WALLS

A direct, but risky, method of attack was for attackers to swarm up huge ladders. It was easy for defenders to shoot climbers or push them off their ladders.

Attackers try to storm the castle using ladders

DESIGN FOR DEFENCE

CASTLES HAD ALL SORTS OF design features
to make them difficult to attack and easy
to defend. Strengthened doors, openings
to shoot through, holes to drop missiles
or pour boiling water on
enemies – all made it hard
for attackers to storm a
medieval castle.

PORTCULLIS
Castles had solid doors made of
wood, reinforced wth metal. There
might also be one or more
portcullises – grilles that could be
lowered in front or behind the door.

*Slots for
observation
and shooting
through*

Timber support

WOODEN HOARDING

HOARDINGS
Wooden hoardings were overhanging structures
built at the top of castle walls, to give defenders
several different lines of fire. Some hoardings had
holes in the floor, enabling defenders to drop
stones or pour boiling water on attackers.

MURDER HOLES
Defenders might seek to trap attackers. They could then kill them by shooting arrows or pouring boiling water through ceiling holes, known as murder holes.

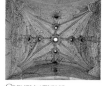

SPIRAL STAIRCASE
Spiral staircases in towers were built to wind clockwise. This gave a right-handed defender plenty of room to swing his sword.

Heavily crenellated Castillo San Marcos

CRENELLATIONS
Crenellations on the top of walls allowed a soldier behind to shoot, while providing protection from enemy fire.

MACHICOLATIONS
Many castles have machicolations – stone parapets jutting from the tops of walls. They have openings through which objects could be dropped on attackers gathered below.

FIRING MISSILES

LOOPHOLES
Narrow loopholes enabled an archer to fire, with little risk of being hit by enemy arrows. The fish-tail shape provides several angles.

EMBRASURES
An embrasure (alcove) provided room for firing. This loophole was designed for firearms.

MOATS AND DITCHES

MOST CASTLES, except those built on high hills, were surrounded by a wet moat or dry ditch. Both provided a barrier against attack, but the moat was the more effective. Moats were usually filled to a depth greater than a man's height.

WATER DEFENCES
Caerphilly Castle, Wales, is surrounded by elaborate water defences consisting of two large lakes and several moats and ditches. A system of tunnels and sluices under the ground allowed the lord to control the water level all the way around the castle.

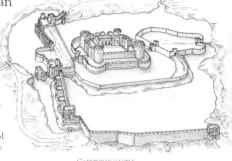

CAERPHILLY CASTLE

CHATEAU DU PLESSIS BOURRÉ
This 15th-century French castle has a moat so large that many of the usual defensive features were thought unnecessary. The moat is crossed by a seven-arched stone bridge.

Castle is still in very good condition

Moat is so wide it looks more like a lake

DRAWBRIDGE

Entry across a moat or ditch was provided by a drawbridge, which was raised to keep attackers out during a seige. The castle at Langeais, France, has twin drawbridges – a large one for horses and carts and a small one for people on foot.

MOAT FACTS

• When there was a moat as well as an earth rampart, the total height from the bottom of the moat to the top of the rampart was at least 9 m (30 ft).

• Moats were sometimes drained and filled in by attackers during a siege.

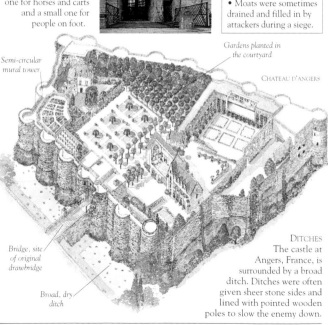

Gardens planted in the courtyard

CHATEAU D'ANGERS

Semi-circular mural tower

Bridge, site of original drawbridge

Broad, dry ditch

DITCHES

The castle at Angers, France, is surrounded by a broad ditch. Ditches were often given sheer stone sides and lined with pointed wooden poles to slow the enemy down.

MEN AND MISSILES

WHEN A CASTLE was attacked, the enemy was usually at a distance, so crossbows and longbows were fired from loopholes around the outer walls. The garrison might also go out on sorties (sudden attacks), picking off as many of the enemy as they could before retreating back inside the castle gates.

WINDLASS
A crossbow was so powerful that some form of machine was needed to pull the cord back ready for firing. A common method of doing this was to use a windlass. This device (left) has handles that the archer turns.

— Windlass cord

WINDLASS

— Stirrup

CROSSBOW
The crossbow fired metal bolts. It was a powerful, deadly weapon, but took time and effort to reload after firing. This was a handicap on the battlefield, but did not matter in a castle, because the archer could hide behind the walls while reloading.

Three spikes rest on the ground

Arrows could fly 300 m (984 ft)

Barbed arrow-head

CALTROPS
Made of iron, caltrops were designed so that one spike pointed upwards when it was thrown on the ground. Defenders scattered them outside the castle gate when an attack was expected. They could badly injure men and horses.

German halberd c.1500

HALBERD
This weapon was used by foot soldiers. Its steel blade could inflict nasty injuries on both men and horses. The halberd could also be used to pull a knight from his horse.

LONGBOW
The longbow was a favourite weapon of English armies from the 14th century onwards. It was light and fast, but required strength from the archer.

LONGBOW

GENERAL PURPOSE

THIN BODKIN

Fragment of shaft

ARROWHEADS
Made of iron, fine-pointed arrowheads came in various shapes. Broad-heads could severely injure horses, bodkins could get through mail; thin bodkins could pierce plate armour.

BROADHEAD

GENERAL PURPOSE

BODKIN

ARCHER FACTS
• Up to 12 arrows could be shot from a longbow in the time it took to load and shoot a single crossbow bolt.

• An archer usually carried 12 arrows, but might shoot others he found on the battlefield.

DECLINE OF THE CASTLE

EUROPEAN SOCIETY became more peaceful during the late 15th century. As a result, nobles looked for more comfortable homes. Warfare was increasingly fought by professional soldiers based in forts, so castles became less important. Some were turned into luxurious palaces. Others fell into disrepair, and their stones were used to construct new buildings.

Walls inside study were covered in green velvet

Chapel's vaulted ceiling sculpted with cockle shells

Tower survives from the 15th-century castle

CHATEAU DE CHENONCEAU

LUXURY CASTLE
This elegant palace was built over the River Cher, France, in the 16th century. It was built in watery surroundings for stunning visual effect rather than for defence. The large windows and lack of crenellations indicate that it is not a true castle.

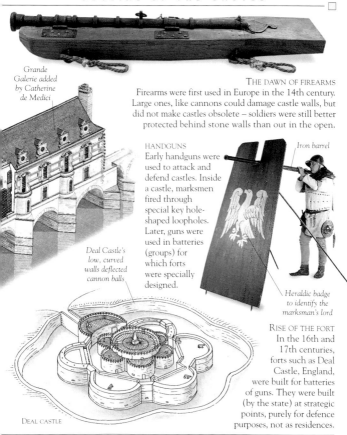

Grande Galerie added by Catherine de Medici

THE DAWN OF FIREARMS

Firearms were first used in Europe in the 14th century. Large ones, like cannons could damage castle walls, but did not make castles obsolete – soldiers were still better protected behind stone walls than out in the open.

HANDGUNS

Early handguns were used to attack and defend castles. Inside a castle, marksmen fired through special key hole-shaped loopholes. Later, guns were used in batteries (groups) for which forts were specially designed.

Iron barrel

Heraldic badge to identify the marksman's lord

Deal Castle's low, curved walls deflected cannon balls

RISE OF THE FORT

In the 16th and 17th centuries, forts such as Deal Castle, England, were built for batteries of guns. They were built (by the state) at strategic points, purely for defence purposes, not as residences.

DEAL CASTLE

DUNGEONS AND PRISONS

AS CASTLES WERE SECURE buildings, they could be used as prisons. This did not happen often, as criminals in the Middle Ages were usually punished by fine or execution. But sometimes political prisoners were held in a castle, or criminals kept there before a trial. Most castles did not have purpose-built dungeons, so prisoners might be held in any secure room.

TORTURE CHAMBER
Torture was unusual in medieval castles, but in later years, the rack was used to force prisoners to reveal military secrets or renounce religious beliefs.

DUNGEON FACTS

• Some dungeons were called *oubliettes*, a French word meaning "locked away and forgotten".

• Many underground vaulted passages thought to be dungeons are actually drains.

IN CHAINS
Very dangerous criminals were not only locked in a cell – they were also restrained by leg irons or a heavy iron collar and chain.

Locking iron collar weighed 16 kg (35 lb)

Heavy iron chain attached to wall

HELD TO RANSOM

Nobles captured in battle were held in a castle until ransom money was paid for their return. They were usually kept in good conditions – a dead prisoner brought no ransom. The Duke of Orléans was held in the Tower of London after the Battle of Agincourt (1415).

THE DUKE OF ORLÉANS HELD TO RANSOM

Stout grille made of hard wood

Wooden peg

Window

BARRED VIEW

In the prison at Loches Castle, France, one cell is entered through a barred door made of solid strips of oak. Inside the cell, a stone bench is the only furniture, and light enters through a small, barred window.

THE PRISON

At Loches, a strong tower next to the keep was used as a prison and torture chamber from the 15th century onwards. The paintings of one 16th-century prisoner, the Duke of Milan, can be seen on the walls of his dark cell.

Part of castle containing prison

CASTLES AROUND THE WORLD

BRITAIN AND IRELAND

WHEN THE NORMANS invaded England in 1066, they
built castles all over the country. Many of their great
towers still survive, often surrounded by later curtain
walls. Castle-building continued throughout the Middle
Ages, with a boom during the 13th century, especially
in the reign of Edward I (1272–1307), who developed
castle design in Wales.

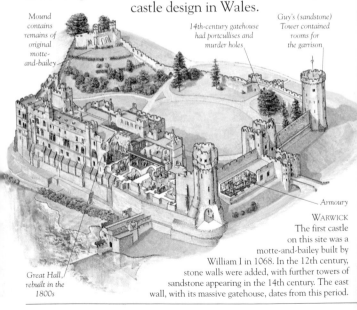

Mound contains remains of original motte-and-bailey

14th-century gatehouse had portcullises and murder holes

Guy's (sandstone) Tower contained rooms for the garrison

Armoury

WARWICK
The first castle
on this site was a
motte-and-bailey built by
William I in 1068. In the 12th century,
stone walls were added, with further towers of
sandstone appearing in the 14th century. The east
wall, with its massive gatehouse, dates from this period.

Great Hall, rebuilt in the 1800s

Low curtain walls, good for firing from, but not for defence

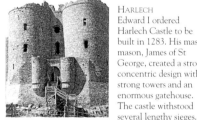

CASTELL-Y-BERE

CASTELL-Y-BERE
This castle was built by the Welsh lord Llwelyn the Great in the 13th century. It has a large, D-shaped tower, typical of Welsh castles. The castle's construction follows the shape of the rock on which it was built.

COLCHESTER

HARLECH
Edward I ordered Harlech Castle to be built in 1283. His master mason, James of St George, created a strong, concentric design with strong towers and an enormous gatehouse. The castle withstood several lengthy sieges.

HARLECH'S GATEHOUSE

COLCHESTER
Britain's largest Norman great tower was built at Colchester, on the foundations of a disused Roman temple. The tower was originally about 27.5 m (90 ft) high, but the top two storeys were pulled down in 1683.

TOWER OF LONDON
This famous royal castle, one of the best-defended in Britain, was begun by the Normans. They built the great tower, called the White Tower, while the surrounding concentric walls were added during the reign of Henry III (1216–72).

TOWER OF LONDON

Scotland

Stone castles were rare in Scotland until the 13th century, but the Scots quickly learned from English and French designs. By the time Edward I of England invaded Scotland in 1296, he had to attack many castles. During the 14th century, the Scottish tower-house emerged.

Crenellated parapet for sentries

TRAQUAIR
Many tower-houses, such as Traquair, were extended to provide more living accommodation. At Traquair, the windows were also enlarged and the battlements demolished to provide extra room in the attic.

NEIDPATH
Tower-houses were built to deter local attacks rather than major assaults. The hall and other living rooms were built one above the other, with crenellations and arrow loops towards the top (above).

EDINBURGH
Once the residence of Scottish kings, this castle was begun in the 6th century on an outcrop of rock overlooking the city. The present buildings date from the 12th to 20th centuries.

EDINBURGH

Ireland

For centuries, the Irish defended themselves with earthworks and wooden ramparts, which often surrounded an entire town. Motte-and-bailey castles were also widely built, hundreds of years after they had fallen out of favour in the rest of Europe. However, many stone castles were also built in Ireland, by English and Norman rulers.

KILKENNY
With its drum towers and tall walls, this castle retains much of its medieval form. The large windows were added much later.

CARRICKFERGUS
Built in the late 12th century by the Anglo-Norman leader John de Coucy, this large castle defends the entrance to Belfast Lough. It has a Norman great tower and a later twin-towered gatehouse.

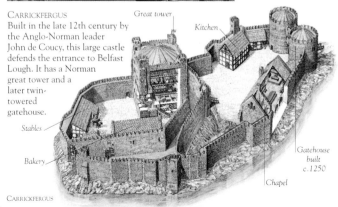

Great tower

Kitchen

Stables

Bakery

Gatehouse built c.1250

Chapel

CARRICKFERGUS

FRANCE

THE COUNTRY that gave Europe feudalism, France is home to some of the earliest castles. Rivalry between the powerful counts of Anjou and Blois led to the building of many castles in the Loire region. The trend continued when England fought France in the Hundred Years' War (1337–1453).

CHATEAU D'AZAY-LE-RIDEAU
During the 1500s, French lords built castles with large windows and comfortable state rooms. At Azay-le-Rideau, built between 1518 and 1527, defensive features were merely decorative.

CHATEAU DE CHINON
The vast structure overlooking the river Vienne is actually three castles. Two were built by the counts of Blois; one, by the counts of Anjou. In the 12th century, Henry II ruled both France and England from Chinon.

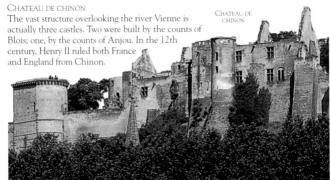

CHATEAU DE CHINON

CHATEAU DE GOULAINE

CHATEAU DE GOULAINE
Goulaine was originally built in the 14th century, but buildings date from the 14th to 17th centuries. It was the scene of a famous siege during the Hundred Years' War, in which the lady of the castle, Yolande de Goulaine, threatened to kill herself if the defenders did not fight off the English.

CHATEAU DE LOCHES

CHATEAU DE LUYNES
The 13th-century castle walls and towers of this castle, built by the first Duke of Luynes, still survive, although they now have large windows. Originally, there would have been crenellations beneath the conical roofs.

CHATEAU DE LUYNES

TOWN OF LOCHES
The ancient 12th-century tower of Loches Castle is typical of early French square keeps. It is surrounded by later curtain walls and mural towers built by French monarch Philip Augustus. These walls were extended around the medieval town.

CHATEAU D'AINAY-LE-VIEIL
This eight-sided courtyard castle retains its 13th-century outer walls, with their arrow slits, crenellations, and massive towers. The gatehouse, guarded by a drawbridge, is also original.

CHATEAU D'AINAY-LE-VIEIL

SCANDINAVIA AND THE LOW COUNTRIES

FEUDALISM CAME LATER to these lands than to the rest of Europe. Castles in Belgium and the Netherlands were the work of feudal lords, while in Scandinavia, kings and church leaders were the main castle builders. Most of these castles are in low-lying regions, so many have water defences. A lack of good building stone in Belgium and the Netherlands meant that castles tended to be built of brick.

VIANDEN

VIANDEN, LUXEMBOURG
One of Europe's smallest countries, Luxembourg, contains one of its largest castles, Vianden. Built in the 11th century, it has a hall that seated 500, and a chapel with a trap-door leading to an underground vault.

MUIDERSLOT

MUIDERSLOT, NETHERLANDS
This rectangular Dutch courtyard castle is surrounded by a moat. Like many castles in the region, it is built of brick. This well-preserved structure dates from the late 14th century, although there has been a castle on the site for around 1,000 years.

KALMAR, SWEDEN

This was one of several castles built to protect the Swedish coast from pirates in the 12th century. Artillery bastions were added in the 16th century. The castle has withstood 20 sieges.

KALMAR

BEERSEL, BELGIUM

Belgium's Beersel Castle was twice captured during a revolt in 1489, at which time it suffered considerable damage. Most of the current castle, with its corner towers, stepped Flemish gables, and broad moat, dates from the rebuild of 1491. The large towers were designed to provide plenty of accommodation.

EGESKOV

BEERSEL

EGESKOV, DENMARK

Built in 1554, this is one of the best-preserved lake-castles. It is built on a foundation of oak piles, rammed down into the mud at the bottom of the lake. Its walls contain secret staircases and embrasures.

GERMANY

MEDIEVAL GERMANY was divided into dozens of tiny independent states, many of which had their own castle. In the 11th century, lords began to build a typically German type of castle with a slender tower, or *Bergfried*, often built on a hilltop. The shape of the castle was thus governed by the site; symmetrically planned castles were rare until the late Middle Ages.

HEIDELBERG
This castle was home to the Counts Palatine of the Rhine valley, who ruled this area in the Middle Ages. Built on a rocky outcrop, it overlooks their capital, the city of Heidelberg. They extended the castle during the Renaissance period.

— Belfry on tower

GERMAN CASTLE FACTS

• The German states were under the general rule of the Holy Roman Emperor; both the emperors and individual rulers built castles.

• The Hohenstaufen family built castles across Germany and Italy (from 1152–1250).

PFALZGRAFENSTEIN
King Ludwig I of Bavaria built this castle in the middle of the river Rhine in 1327. Pflazgrafenstein was originally intended as a base for officials collecting tolls from ships on the river.

BURG ELTZ

When a German noble family grew, several brothers could inherit a castle and divide it among them. This type of castle was called a *Ganerbenburg*. Burg Eltz was occupied by six branches of its ruling family, each of which had homes around the courtyard.

BURG ELTZ

Bergfried

LICHTENSTEIN

LICHTENSTEIN

Three branches of the same family lived in this castle, resulting in an irregular mixture of buildings clustered around its *Bergfried*. Access was by way of a wooden bridge.

MARKSBURG

MARKSBURG

The Marksburg is typical of many German castles that grew gradually over the centuries. It was begun in the 13th century, when the tall tower was built on a high crag above the Rhine. The courtyard was added in the 14th century.

CENTRAL AND EASTERN EUROPE

LIKE GERMANY, MUCH OF THIS AREA was part of the Holy Roman Empire during the Middle Ages, and natural features such as hilltops and crags were used to enhance fortifications. In low-lying areas, water defences were popular, and many castles were built near lakes.

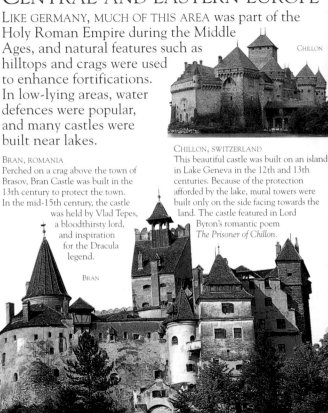

CHILLON

CHILLON, SWITZERLAND
This beautiful castle was built on an island in Lake Geneva in the 12th and 13th centuries. Because of the protection afforded by the lake, mural towers were built only on the side facing towards the land. The castle featured in Lord Byron's romantic poem *The Prisoner of Chillon.*

BRAN, ROMANIA
Perched on a crag above the town of Brasov, Bran Castle was built in the 13th century to protect the town. In the mid-15th century, the castle was held by Vlad Tepes, a bloodthirsty lord, and inspiration for the Dracula legend.

BRAN

MARIENBURG, POLAND
This is one of several
castles built by the
religious military
order, the Teutonic
Knights, in the 14th
century. It has several
typical features,
being a brick-built
courtyard
type with a
large chapel.

MARIENBURG

DÜRNSTEIN

DÜRNSTEIN, AUSTRIA
Richard I of England was held prisoner
at Dürnstein on his return from the
Third Crusade. The castle had two
walls, one at the bottom of the cliff on
which it stands, the other half-way up.
Some of the walls were destroyed by
mining in the 13th century.

KARLSTEJN, CZECH REPUBLIC
Originally built in the 14th century
by Charles of Hungary, this
castle near Prague
combines strength
and elegance.
Built on a craggy
hill, its massive
keep was protected
by five large
towers and high
curtain walls.

SPAIN

FOR MUCH OF THE MIDDLE AGES, Christians fought the Moors (Muslims) for control of Spain. Both sides built castles and copied each other's ideas on fortification. The Moors liked to build square or wedge-shaped enclosures. The Christians introduced the great tower, or *torre del homenaje* (tower of homage).

Torre del homenaje usually had pointed roofs

ALCÁZAR OF SEGOVIA
In the 11th century, the Christians took Segovia from the Moors and built this stronghold. It is in the form of a *gran buque* (great ship) castle, a long building, tapering towards one end.

Pointed crenellations

CASTILLO DE COCA
This castle is built of brick – even the moat has a brick lining. It was constructed for Alfonso de Fonseca, Christian archbishop of Seville, but has many examples of Moorish motifs.

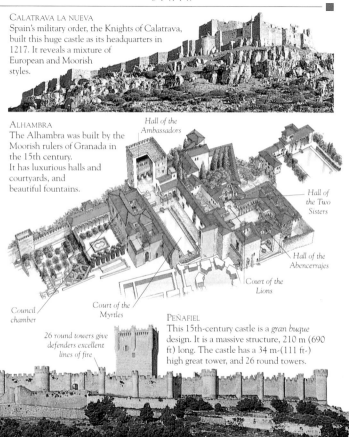

CALATRAVA LA NUEVA
Spain's military order, the Knights of Calatrava, built this huge castle as its headquarters in 1217. It reveals a mixture of European and Moorish styles.

ALHAMBRA
The Alhambra was built by the Moorish rulers of Granada in the 15th century. It has luxurious halls and courtyards, and beautiful fountains.

Hall of the Ambassadors

Hall of the Two Sisters

Hall of the Abencerrajes

Court of the Lions

Council chamber

Court of the Myrtles

PEÑAFIEL
This 15th-century castle is a *gran buque* design. It is a massive structure, 210 m (690 ft) long. The castle has a 34 m-(111 ft-) high great tower, and 26 round towers.

26 round towers give defenders excellent lines of fire

ITALY

IN THE MIDDLE AGES, Italy was made up of small independent states, often based around fortified towns. As time went by, lords strengthened the walls of their town homes, creating Italy's first true castles. Some had a great tower with curtain walls. Others were courtyard castles with heavy wall towers. Holy Roman Emperor, Frederick II, built many castles in Italy during the 13th century.

CASTEL SANT'ANGELO, ROME
Raised on the site of Roman buildings, this great fortress was extended throughout the Middle Ages. Once home to the city's chief noble family, it was later taken over by the popes, who lived there during times of unrest.

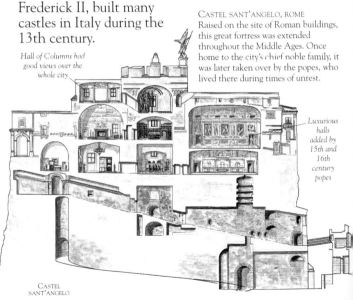

Hall of Columns had good views over the whole city

Luxurious halls added by 15th and 16th century popes

CASTEL SANT'ANGELO

SAN GIMIGNANO TOWERS

In this small Italian town, rival families built a total of 72 towers, 14 of which are still standing.

Rival lords showed off by building towers taller and taller

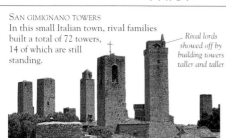

CASTEL DEL MONTE

Frederick II chose an unusual octagonal design for Castel del Monte in southern Italy. The castle, begun in 1240, is fortified with thick walls and eight turrets for archers. The rooms inside were once very luxurious.

Octagonal satellite tower   *Octagonal courtyard*

FLOOR PLAN

The plan of Castel del Monte shows eight vaulted rooms, one on each octagonal face.

CASTEL NUOVO, NAPLES

Remodelled by Alfonso I of Aragon who used both Spanish and Italian builders, this castle has a triumphal arch, built to commemorate Alfonso's entry into Naples in 1443.

CASTEL NUOVO

THE MIDDLE EAST

CRUSADERS WERE IMPRESSED by the huge Byzantine and Muslim fortifications they encountered on their expeditions, and took over these strongholds to encourage European settlers. They built castles to guard roads and to help them attack nearby towns. By the late 12th century, such castles were being used as border posts, administrative centres, and army bases.

QATRANA, JORDAN
Qatrana is a typical Muslim fortress. Its plain, rectangular walls were difficult to attack. The castle was protected with arrow slits, pointed crenellations along the tops of the wall, and machicolations above the doorway.

VAN, TURKEY
Many Middle Eastern castles were used by different peoples as the area passed from one ruling power to another. Van Castle in Turkey was first built during the Byzantine period, in 850. In the Middle Ages, the Seljuk Turks took it over and extended it, and they were followed by the Ottoman Turks. Armenian Christians later lived in the castle.

Thick curtain wall surrounds main tower

Rocky outcrop is difficult to scale

Square, main tower

KERAK, JORDAN
Built by crusaders in 1142, Kerak is located near routes used by Muslim traders and pilgrims. Its garrison, led by their lord, Reynald de Chatillon, frequently raided passers-by. This infuriated the Muslims, who laid siege to Kerak in 1183 and 1184. The final siege in 1188 lasted eight months and led to the fall of the castle.

CRUSADER CASTLES

• More than 40 crusader castles were built along the coastal strip of the eastern Mediterranean.

• Many castles had huge store rooms: the defenders of Baghras Castle, Turkey, stowed away 12,000 sacks of grain in case of siege.

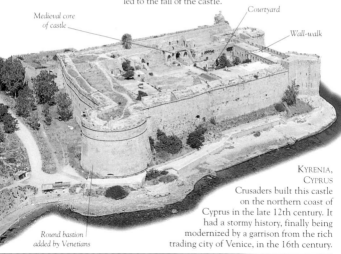

Medieval core of castle

Courtyard

Wall-walk

Round bastion added by Venetians

KYRENIA, CYPRUS
Crusaders built this castle on the northern coast of Cyprus in the late 12th century. It had a stormy history, finally being modernized by a garrison from the rich trading city of Venice, in the 16th century.

Krak des Chevaliers

Krak des Chevaliers (Castle of the Knights), in Syria, was built by the Knights Hospitaller. The knights lived like monks, but took up arms in defence of crusaders or Christian pilgrims. Thought by T.E. Lawrence (Lawrence of Arabia) to be "the best preserved and most admirable castle in the world", Krak withstood Saracen attacks until 1271. It only fell because the garrison was tricked into surrender by the Sultan Beibars.

Strong, round tower

Commander's headquarters

Aqueduct brought water into the castle

CRUSADERS' STRONGHOLD
Krak began life as a Muslim fortress, which French crusaders took over in the 12th century. They rebuilt it, constructing reservoirs, and a mill for grinding corn.

TOWERS
Most of Krak's towers are round, to prevent mining, although there was little risk of this owing to the castle's rocky foundations.

Main hall was used for meals and meetings

A strict religious order, the Hospitallers had a large chapel

PLAN
A plan of the castle shows two lines of concentric walls, with a narrow entrance that was easy to defend. The hall, chapel and commander's room are in the heart of the castle.

Wall towers gave good vantage points

Batter (slope) makes walls difficult to scale

Dark passage

ENTRANCE
The castle entrance is overlooked by battlements and arrow slits. Even if an enemy got past these, he was faced with a walk along a narrow, covered passageway that bent back on itself. This was kept dark, so that attackers would be almost blinded as they emerged into the light of the courtyard.

Arrow-slits were placed all around walls

JAPAN

IN THE 16TH AND 17TH CENTURIES, a political system developed in Japan that was very similar to European feudalism. Local lords built large castles to provide security during periods of political unrest. These castles had tall wooden towers with overhanging roofs. The towers were set in stone-walled courtyards that often had many inner walls and side towers, so that enemies could be trapped there and kept away from the main tower.

MATSUMOTO

HIMEJI

Outer courtyard is intended to trap enemy

MATSUMOTO

This 16th-century castle has a vast wooden tower and side towers. Galleries run around each floor, protected by wooden shutters. The lord favoured archers, because their weapons were silent, so the walls have narrow slits.

NIJO

Castles like Nijo, which dates from 1603, were built using a framework of strong wooden beams. The dimensions were carefully worked out, giving Japanese castles an elegance often lacking in their European counterparts. The luxurious interior of Nijo is decorated with landscape paintings.

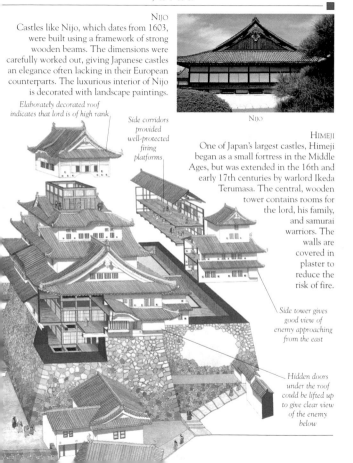

NIJO

HIMEJI

One of Japan's largest castles, Himeji began as a small fortress in the Middle Ages, but was extended in the 16th and early 17th centuries by warlord Ikeda Terumasa. The central, wooden tower contains rooms for the lord, his family, and samurai warriors. The walls are covered in plaster to reduce the risk of fire.

Elaborately decorated roof indicates that lord is of high rank

Side corridors provided well-protected firing platforms

Side tower gives good view of enemy approaching from the east

Hidden doors under the roof could be lifted up to give clear view of the enemy below

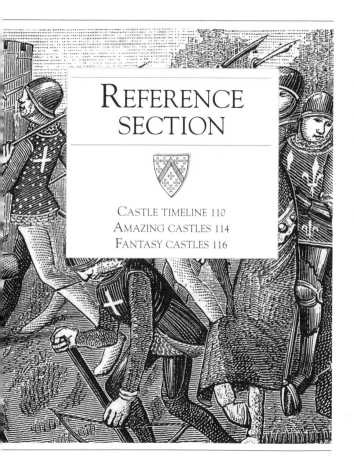

REFERENCE SECTION

CASTLE TIMELINE

THIS TIMELINE traces the development of castles
and castle warfare. Castle design changed greatly,
from simple wooden tower with enclosure and ditch,
to massive stone tower surrounded by walls and moat.
Castles were later superseded by the palace and fort.

476–864	911–1037
•476 End of the Roman empire.	•911 Rollo, Viking chieftain, settles in northwestern France; his followers become the first Normans.
•c.700 Introduction of stirrups to Europe from Asia helps horsemen fight from the saddle.	•c.950 Earliest-known stone tower is built at Doué-la-Fontaine, France.
•c.800 The emperors of the Carolingian empire defend their realm from Viking and Magyar invasions with mounted cavalrymen – the first knights. Feudalism develops in Europe.	•987–1040 Foulques Nerra, Count of Anjou, builds 27 castles as part of his campaign against the Count of Blois.
	•c.1000 The Normans start to build castles in many parts of Europe; they favour motte-and-bailey designs and strong, stone great towers.
•c.800–1150 The Romanesque style of architecture is fashionable in Europe. Typical Romanesque features appearing on castles include semi-circular arches, round-headed windows, and barrel vaults. In England, the Romanesque style is often called "Norman".	•1000–1200 Italian towns, such as Florence, Rome, and Venice, become independent city states.
•864 Charles the Bald, ruler of the western part of the Carolingian empire, orders that castles built without his consent be destroyed.	•1037 Fernando of Castile conquers the kingdom of León, northern Spain, greatly extending Christian power in the area.

CAROLINGIAN KNIGHT

MOTTE-AND-BAILEY

1066–1113	1118–1180
•1066 William of Normandy invades England and builds castles all over the country. •1095 The crusading movement begins; Europeans build castles in the Holy Land. They also bring back Eastern ideas about fortification to Europe. •c.1100 Tower keeps become increasingly common in much of Europe. STONE TOWER Archers become important in warfare. •1100 German lords begin to build tall, slender towers (*Bergfrieder*), often sited on high, craggy hills for natural defence. BATTERING RAM •1100–1200 Simple siege engines, such as battering rams and siege towers, are used to attack castles. •1113 The Knights of St John, or Knights Hospitaller, are founded in Jerusalem. They protect Christian pilgrims, and fight on behalf of crusader kingdoms in the eastern Mediterranean. They build some of the most notable castles in the area.	•1118 The Knights Templar are founded to protect Christian pilgrims in Palestine. Their name comes from the fact that their first house was built on the site of the Temple in Jerusalem. •1140s European crusaders build several castles in the eastern Mediterranean; the most common design is a rectangle with a tower at each corner. •1142 Crusaders take over Krak des Chevaliers in Syria. KRAK DES CHEVALIERS •1150–1500 The Gothic style of architecture becomes fashionable in Europe. This style is typified by pointed arches and ribbed vaults. •1160 Henry II of England experiments with new tower designs, including the many-sided keep at Orford, Suffolk. •1169 First Norman invasion of Ireland finds the Irish relying on walled towns and wooden fortifications. •1180–1226 Reign of Philip Augustus of France, who builds many castles.

1190–1270	1270–1337
•1190 The Teutonic Order of Knights is founded in Germany to defend Christian lands in Syria and Palestine. They build many castles, especially in eastern Europe.	•1270–1350 Concentric plans become fashionable, and curtain walls of many castles are strengthened.

•1190s Courtyard castles increase in popularity, as the focus of defence shifts away from the great tower and towards stronger walls and gatehouses.

•1196–8 Richard I builds Chateau-Gaillard in France; the castle, one of the strongest to date, pioneered the use of inner and outer defences that were designed to work together.

•1200s Rounded wall towers begin to be built, and brick castles appear in the Netherlands.

TOWER AT PEMBROKE

•1220–1250 Reign of the Holy Roman Emperor Frederick II, who builds numerous castles in Germany and Italy, and experiments with new designs.

•1266 Siege of Kenilworth Castle, England, lasts six months – one of the longest sieges on record.

•1270s Machicolations begin to replace wooden hoardings.

•1271 Krak des Chevaliers falls to the Muslims (Saracens).

•1272–1307 Reign of Edward I of England, who is well known for his castle building in Wales.

•1291 End of the Crusades.

BEAUMARIS CASTLE

• 1300s Emergence of the Scottish tower house.

•1304 More sophisticated siege machines, such as catapults, become widespread.

•1320s Cannons first used in Europe.

•1330 Plate armour in widespread use.

14TH-CENTURY GAUNTLET

•1337–1453 The Hundred Years' War between France and England stimulates castle building and developments in warfare.

1347 – 1453	1476 – 1900

• 1347–51 The Black Death kills 25 million people across Europe.

• 1380s Gunloops first built into castles, as at Carisbrooke, Isle of Wight, England.

GUNLOOP

• 1400s Castle building in decline in Europe.

• 1415 At the Battle of Agincourt, English longbowmen triumph over the French; mounted knights begin to decline in importance on the battlefield.

• 1418 The English besiege Chateau-Gaillard, France, for 16 months; the garrison finally surrenders owing to lack of water.

LONGBOW ARCHER

• 1450 Many castles walls are made thicker to cope with the destructive power of artillery.

• 1453 Ottoman Turks capture the city of Constantinople (modern Istanbul), bringing the Byzantine empire to an end.

HAND GUNNER

• 1476–7 In the wars between France and Burgundy, pikemen and hand gunners win many victories over knights.

• 1492 Spain's Christian rulers, Ferdinand and Isabella, conquer Granada, the last bastion of the Moors. This completes the Christian reconquest of Spain.

• 1500s Comfortable palaces take precedence over castles across Europe.

• 1509–1547 Reign of Henry VIII of England, who builds forts (such as Deal and Walmer castles) to defend England from possible invasion; no one lives in these buildings, which are essentially firing-platforms.

• c.1600 Great age of castle building in Japan.

HIMEJI

• 1600s French military genius Sebastian le Prestre de Vauban designs star-shaped forts.

• 1800s Renewed interest in castles as symbols of the medieval world. Ludwig II, the "mad" king of Bavaria, builds his "fairy-tale" castles in Germany.

AMAZING CASTLES

SINCE MEDIEVAL TIMES, castles have witnessed countless
thrilling events – sieges, executions, ghostly visitations
– and many strange tales are told concerning them.
Here are a few of the most intriguing.

WORLD'S LARGEST CASTLE
The largest ancient castle in the world
is Hradcany Castle, in Prague, Czech
Republic. It was originally constructed
in the 9th century, and has retained
churches, chapels, halls, and towers from
every period of its history.
The castle covers about
8 hectares (20 acres).

HRADCANY CASTLE

LEFT TO ROT
During the 13th century, Templar
Knights were imprisoned in Chinon
Castle, in France. They were left to
starve, and the castle walls still bear the
writings of the knights facing their doom.

DEATH BY RED-HOT POKER
Berkeley Castle, England, is famous for
the ghastly murder of Edward II by order
of his wife. While he was sleeping, a
red-hot poker was forced into his bowels.

THE GREY LADY OF GLAMIS
Glamis Castle, Scotland, is said to be
one of the world's most haunted castles.
Among its ghosts are the cruel "Earl
Beardie", a tongueless woman, a lady in
white, and a Grey Lady, thought to be
Lady Glamis who was burned alive as a
witch at Edinburgh over 400 years ago.

LOVE TRIANGLE
Two ghosts are reported to haunt the
magnificent Chateau de Chenonceau,
France. Catherine de Medici, wife of
Henry II, reappears under a full
moon, combing the hair of her
rival, Diane de Poitiers, the
king's beautiful mistress.
When Henry died his
jealous wife exiled
Diane from the
chateau, the one place
she truly loved.
Diane's sad ghost is
seen, at the time of
the full moon,
standing before
the great mirror
in her bedroom.

DIANE'S GHOST

DREAM CASTLE

Neuschwanstein Castle in Germany was one of several fantastic castles created by King Ludwig II of Bavaria, who ruled his country, reluctantly, from 1864 to 1886. Inspired by Wagner's operas, the castle was designed by a Munich scene painter, and built to look like a medieval castle, although it was a lot more luxurious inside. Walt Disney's famous castle logo was inspired by this castle.

NEUSCHWANSTEIN

MAGICAL KISS

It is said that whoever kisses the magical stone at Blarney Castle, Ireland, will acquire magical eloquence. The stone is set in the wall below the castle battlements. In order to kiss it, a visitor is grasped by the feet and suspended backwards under the parapet.

TALL STORY?

According to legend, when Richard I of England was imprisoned in Dürnstein Castle, Austria, for over a year, his minstrel, Blondel, searched for him everywhere. He sat outside castle walls and sang Richard's favourite songs. Eventually, he heard the king join in, and realized that he had found his lord.

GREAT ESCAPES

Colditz Castle, Germany, stands on a great rock overlooking the Mulde river. Dating back to 1028, it has many secret passages that were used in sieges. During World War II, it was a high-security prisoner camp. Though the castle was allegedly escape-proof, a number of Allied prisoners managed to get out.

PRINCES IN THE TOWER

English king Richard III was said to have ordered the murder of his nephews, Edward V and Richard, in the Tower of London in 1483. The princes were kept there to prevent nobles from trying to put Edward on the throne. Who really killed them, and when, is a mystery.

TOWER OF TERROR

The Tower of London was a royal residence, armoury, treasury, and a prison for enemies of the crown. Many were brought by boat from trial at Westminster Hall to the infamous entrance, Traitors' Gate. Notorious traitors were executed on nearby Tower Hill, and their heads displayed on poles as a grim warning to others who might challenge the sovereign.

HEADS ON POLES

FANTASY CASTLES

CASTLES PROVIDE spectacular settings for many romantic legends and swashbuckling tales. In fairy tales, castles are often enchanted places where dwell demons, orgres, or captive princesses. Some novelists portray them as sinister places fraught with terrors.

CAMELOT

CAMELOT
King Arthur's magical castle and court was known as Camelot. From here the noble knights of the Round Table rode forth to find the Holy Grail. Various British locations have been suggested as the possible site of this mythical castle. They include Caerleon Castle in Wales, Tintagel in Cornwall, and Cadbury Hill in Somerset.

SCOTT'S ROMANTIC NOVELS
The Scottish novelist, Sir Walter Scott, wrote about the lives of castle dwellers in his swash-buckling novels, *Ivanhoe* (1820), *Kenilworth* (1821), and *Castle Dangerous* (1831). Based on historical events, the books feature some real-life figures as characters.

EPIC POEMS
During the Middle Ages, poets wrote long, narrative poems that glorified chivalric behaviour. The French *Song of Roland* and the Spanish *Poem of the Cid* are both about knights in the time of feudalism. They tell of the storming of castles and wars against the Moors.

SHAKESPEARE'S CASTLE DRAMAS
Much of the action in Shakespeare's plays takes place in castles. The murder of King Duncan in *Macbeth* (c.1608) occurs at Glamis Castle, Scotland. *Hamlet* (c.1608) is set at Kronborg castle in Denmark, known as Elsinore in the play. Hamlet first sees the terrifying ghost of his murdered father, the king of Denmark, whilst walking on the castle battlements. The ghost urges Hamlet to avenge the foul crime by killing the murderer – Claudius, Hamlet's own uncle.

HAMLET

CHATEAU D' USSÉ

SLEEPING BEAUTY
Built in 1462 as a castle and later ornamented with turrets, towers, and windows, the Chateau d'Ussé inspired Charles Perrault to write *The Sleeping Beauty*. It overlooks the River Indre in western France. Other fairy tales, such as *Puss in Boots*, and *Beauty and the Beast* feature enchanted castles with strange or sinister occupants.

GOTHIC CASTLE STORIES
Regarded as the first Gothic novel, Horace Walpole's *Castle of Otranto* (1764), is set in 12th-century Italy. It pits the villain Manfred against an innocent heroine, Isabella. In film adaptations of Mary Shelley's novel, *Frankenstein* (1818), the setting for the scientist's monstrous experiments is a remote castle. In *The Pit and the Pendulum* (1843), by Edgar Allen Poe, a prisoner of the Spanish Inquisition is held at Toledo Castle. He awaits death by a razor-sharp swinging pendulum in a rat-infested dungeon.

FORBIDDEN ROOMS
A castle's secret rooms and nooks and crannies make it a mysterious place. In the Finnish fairy tale *The Heart's Door*, a young man is given the keys to 24 extraordinary rooms in a copper castle. He is told that he can enter the 24th room "at his own risk". Curiosity gets the better of him and he unlocks the door. Inside he finds a lovely woman, but the path of true love is not smooth.

BLUEBEARD
In the French story *Bluebeard*, the contents of a secret chamber are not as agreeable. Bluebeard's new wife is forbidden access to "the little room". When she peers inside, she sees the bodies of her husband's former wives. The same fate now beckons her.

DRACULA

DRACULA'S CASTLE
One of the classic horror stories, Bram Stoker's *Dracula* (1897), would not be the same without its sinister castle setting. The story was inspired by the cruelties of the sadistic Transylvanian prince Vlad Tepes or "Vlad the Impaler" (1430–1476). Based at Bran Castle, he reigned for less than ten years, yet his insatiable lust for blood may have caused at least 50,000 deaths.

Resources

Tourist Information Centres can give you information about national or local castles, particularly those open to the public. Museums are another useful source. Staff there may be able to tell you about the history of local castles. Some may exhibit medieval artifacts.

ORGANIZATIONS

English Heritage
Customer Services
429 Oxford Street
London, W1R 2HD
English Heritage is responsible for many English castles. As well as providing information, it operates a membership scheme, with free admission to properties for all members.

Friends of Historic Scotland
Room 214
20 Brandon Street
Edinburgh, EH3 5RA
Many Scottish castles are in the care of Historic Scotland. Members of English Heritage are given free admission to these properties.

Cadw: Welsh Historic Monuments
Brunel House
2 Fitzalan Road
Cardiff, CF2 1UF
Many Welsh castles are in the care of Cadw. Members of English Heritage are given free admission to these properties.

National Trust
36 Queen Anne's Gate
London, SW1H 9AS
This charity preserves buildings and areas of countryside. The trust owns several castles in England.

MUSEUMS

British Museum
Great Russell Street
London, WC1B 3DG
Britain's national museum provides historical background information on the Middle Ages.

Museum of London
London Wall
London, EC2 5HN
Modern museum covering the history of the capital: includes much information about the medieval period relevant to the history of the castle.

Royal Armouries
Armouries Drive
Leeds
West Yorkshire, LS10 1LT
Houses one of the finest collections of arms and armour in the world.

CASTLES TO VISIT

BRITAIN
Tower of London
London
Famous royal castle with Norman White Tower. Houses the Crown Jewels, ravens, and other exhibits.

Dover Castle
Dover
Huge castle with large tower and later curtain walls; hosts events in which medieval warfare,

jousting, and scenes from daily life are re-enacted.

Warwick Castle
Warwick
Magnificent fortress with state rooms, armoury and wax figures to illustrate its history.

IRELAND
Blarney Castle
Blarney
Famous for the Blarney Stone which visitors can kiss. Little remains of the castle except the keep.

FRANCE
Chateau de Loches
Loches
Medieval town with magnificent castle boasting the deepest dungeons in the Loire.

Chateau de Saumur
Saumur
Celebrated fairy-tale chateau with guided tour.

Chateau de Chenonceau
Chenonceau
Lavish chateau and gardens

stretching across the river Cher.

ITALY
Castel del Monte
Località Andria, Bari
One of the most sophisticated secular buildings of the European Middle Ages.

Castel Sant'Angelo
Rome
From dank cells to fine apartments of Renaissance popes, the castle museum cover all aspects of the site's history.

GERMANY
Neuschwanstein
Füssen
Famous fairy-tale castle in the Bavarian mountains. Luxurious rooms are open to the public.

Burg Eltz
Münstermaifeld
Spectacular castle set in woods. Guided tours show original furnishings, wall hangings, and paintings.

SPAIN
Alhambra
Granada
A magical use of space, light, water, and decoration characterizes this sumptuous palace.

Alcázar of Segovia
Segovia
Spectacular castle built on rocky outcrop, with typical Spanish design features.

CZECH REPUBLIC
Hradcany
Prague
Still housing a presidential office, this huge castle has galleries and museums.

ROMANIA
Bran
Bran
A superb medieval castle and home of the Dracula legend.

SWEDEN
Kalmar
Kalmar
This magnificent 13th-century coastal castle has survived 20 sieges.

Glossary

ARTILLERY
Firearms, such as handguns and cannons.

ASHLAR
Building stone precisely cut and finished to a smooth surface.

BAILEY
Castle courtyard usually associated with a motte.

BAILIFF
Person in charge of allotting work to peasants, organizing repairs to castles, and doing other jobs on a medieval estate.

BALLISTA
Siege engine taking the form of a giant crossbow.

BARBICAN
Outlying defence, usually in the form of a walled courtyard protecting a castle gate.

BARREL VAULT
Tunnel-like (barrel-shaped), semi-circular stone ceiling.

BARTIZAN
Corner turret projecting from a high wall, popular in Spanish castles.

BASINET
Close-fitting medieval soldier's helmet, with a visor.

BASTION
Tower projecting from castle wall.

BATTERING RAM
Large beam used to break down the walls or doors of a fortification.

BATTLEMENT
Parapet on top of a castle wall, with a series of gaps, allowing defenders to shoot through; alternative term for crenellation.

BERGFRIED
Type of German castle with a slender tower.

BREWHOUSE
Building or room where ale was brewed.

BUTTERY
Chamber used for storing and preparing food and drink.

CAROLINGIAN EMPIRE
Dynasty that ruled in France and Germany from 751–987.

CHATEAU
French word for castle; now often used to describe a country or manor house.

CHIVALRY
Medieval principles of knighthood.

CITADEL
Stronghold within, or close to, a city.

CONCENTRIC CASTLE
Castle with two or more concentric (with the same centre) walls.

CONSTABLE
Official put in charge of a castle while his lord was away. Also known as a castellan.

COURTYARD
Walled enclosure containing a great hall and other buildings.

COURTYARD CASTLE
Type of castle consisting of a courtyard and a stone curtain wall.

CRENELLATION
Battlements on top
of a castle wall.

CROSSBOW
Weapon with a bow
arranged at a right-angle
to a wooden stock; it was
used to fire metal bolts.

CURTAIN WALL
Outer wall of a castle.

DESMENE
Area of land reserved
for a lord.

DIVIDERS
Instrument with two
pointed arms, used
for measuring or
dividing lines.

DONJON
Another name for great
tower or keep.

DRAWBRIDGE
Lifting bridge that
can be raised to keep
out an enemy.

DRUM TOWER
Semi-circular or
rounded tower.

DUBBING
Ceremony in which
a monarch or high-
ranking lord gives
another person the
title of knight; usually
involved tapping a new
knight on each shoulder
with a sword.

EARTHWORK
Fortification made of
earth mounds, banks,
and ditches.

EMBRASURE
Alcove in inner wall
where archers can
load their weapons
and fire.

ENCLOSURE
Castle courtyard.

FALCONRY
The practice of keeping
falcons and training
them to hunt. Now a
sport, in medieval times,
falconry was used as a
way of hunting.

FEUDALISM
Social system
operating in the
Middle Ages, according
to which land was
granted to nobles in
return for services.

FOREBUILDING
Structure or building
protruding from the
front of a great tower,
containing the
entrance and, often,
the chapel.

FORT
Fortification designed
to protect defenders
who did not usually
live there.

GANERBENBURG
German castle divided
into several dwelling
units, each occupied
by a different branch
of a family.

GARDEROBE
Lavatory.

GARRISON
The soldiers who
manned and occupied
a castle.

GATEHOUSE
The entrance building
in a curtain wall;
usually one of the most
heavily fortified parts of
a castle.

GAUNTLET
Armoured glove, often
with long cuff.

GRAN BUQUE
Type of Spanish castle
in the shape of a ship.

GREAT TOWER
Main tower of a castle,
often containing a hall,
a lord's private
chambers, store rooms;
also known as a keep.

HALL
Main reception room
of a castle, used for
meals, meetings, and
formal occasions. It
also served as a sleeping
area for servants.·

HERALDRY
The system of coats of arms used to identify noble families.

HOARDING
Timber structure projecting from the top of a wall, used as a firing platform.

JOUST
Combat, put on for entertainment, in which two knights rode towards each other with lances.

KEEP
Alternative name for great tower.

KNIGHT
Man who served his lord as a mounted warrior.

LONGBOW
Large, powerful wooden bow, used to shoot arrows, often over long distances.

LOOPHOLE
Narrow opening through which defenders could shoot.

LORD
Any male member of the nobility or knighthood, often holder of a castle or manor.

MACHILOCATION
Projecting stone structure on top of wall from which defenders could drop missiles on those below.

MAIL
(OR CHAIN MAIL)
Flexible armour made of interlocking metal rings.

MANACLE
Lockable metal ring used to secure the hands of a prisoner.

MANGONEL
Siege engine in the form of a stone-throwing catapult.

MASON
Skilled stoneworker.

MILITARY ORDER
Organized group of fighting monks, who took religious vows but also took part in certain types of warfare.

MINING
Tunnelling under a castle wall in order to weaken the foundations and bring the castle down.

MOORS
The Muslim ruling class of Spain during the Middle Ages.

MOTTE
Natural or man-made mound on which a castle was built.

MOTTE-AND-BAILEY
Wooden castle based on an earth mound and an adjoining courtyard.

MURAL TOWER
Tower projecting from the curtain wall of a castle.

MURDER HOLE
Opening in ceiling through which defenders could fire or drop missiles on enemies below.

OUBLIETTE
Dungeon, often reached by a trapdoor in a floor.

PAGE
Young boy of noble birth who served in the household of a lord, and sometimes became a squire.

PALISADE
Strong wooden fence.

PARAPET
The wall protecting the outer side of a wall-walk.

PEWTER
Metal alloy, often containing tin, lead, and copper.

PIKEMAN
Soldier carrying a pike or similar long-handled weapon.

PLATE ARMOUR
Armour made of jointed metal plates.

PORTCULLIS
Grille that could be lowered at a castle gate to keep out enemies or trap them in a gatehouse.

POTTAGE
Thick soup.

RAMPARTS
Earth banks surrounding a castle.

REEVE
Peasant appointed as supervisor of work on the lord's land.

RIBBED VAULT
Stone ceiling with a supporting network of protruding stone structures called ribs.

RINGWORK
Round castle consisting of a circular rampart and wooden fence, protecting a slightly raised courtyard.

SAMURAI
Japanese mounted warrior.

SHELL KEEP
Round stone structure containing lean-to buildings, erected on a castle motte.

SHERIFF
Royal official, based in a castle, who was in charge of law and order.

SIEGE ENGINE
Large weapon or device, such as a battering ram or big catapult, used to attack a castle.

SIEGE TOWER
Wooden tower on wheels which attackers used to climb over castle walls.

SMITH
Person who worked with metal.

SQUIRE
Young man who served a knight, helping him with his horses and armour, who hoped to become a knight himself.

STEWARD
Official in charge of the running of a lord's estate; managing work, keeping accounts, etc.

TORRE DEL HOMENJA
Spanish term for great tower or keep.

TOURNAMENT
Event featuring jousts and mock battles held for entertainment and as practice for warfare.

TOURNEY
Mock battle staged as part of a tournament.

TOWER-HOUSE
Form of small castle, common in Scotland, consisting mainly or entirely of a single tower.

TROUBADOUR
Poet-musician of the Middle Ages, especially one who specialized in songs of courtly love.

TURRET
Small tower sticking out from a wall, often containing a staircase.

VAULT
Arched structure that forms ceiling.

VISOR
Flap on a helmet that can be pulled down to protect the face.

WALL-WALK
Path along the top of a castle wall.

WINDLASS
Winding mechanism, such as that used to load a crossbow.

Index

Acknowledgements

Dorling Kindersley would like to thank:
Hilary Bird for the index; Chateau de Saumur,
Cotswold Farm Park, Gordon Models, Chateau de
Loches, Museum of St John, Order of The Black
Prince, Pitt Rivers Museum; Caroline Potts for
picture library services; Tanya Tween for design
assistance and special photography by Jerry Young.
Robert Graham and Natasha Billing for research.

Illustrations by:
Janet Allis, David Ashby, Stephen Biesty, Joanna
Cameron, Brian Craker, John Crawford-Fraser,
Paolo Danati, Brian Delf, Peter Dennis, Will
Giles/Sandra Pond, Chris Orr, Kevin Robinson,
Nick Shewring, Mike Taylor, Eric Thomas.

Photographs by:
Max Alexander, Peter Anderson, Geoff Brightling,
Joe Cornish, Geoff Dann, Mike Dunning, Steve
Gorton, Paul Harris, John Heseltine, Alan Hills,
Paul Kenward, Dave King, Neil Lukas, Liz
Macaulay, Steven Oliver, John Parker, Martin
Plomer, Rob Reichenfeld, Dave Rudkin, Tim
Ridley, Kim Sayer, Micheal J. Waterman.

Picture credits:
T=top b=bottom c=centre l=left r=right
Hunting Aerofilms Ltd: 23tc, 23cl. AKG London:
59tr. The Ancient Art and Architecture
Collection Ltd: 12cl, 15tr, 55tl, 60tl, 61br, 68bl,
96tr, 97cl, 102b, 107tl. The Bridgeman Art Library:
British Library/Bridgeman Art Library London:
16br building Marseilles, 32br Archbishop of
Arundel, 33br June mowing, 35tl Le Rustican du
Cultivement des Terres, 37tr Christine De Pisan,
39br Lydgate and the Canterbury pilgrims, 40-41,
42br 15th-century battle, 50cr lady and her lover,
56-57 tapestry Dukes of York, 62bc roasting spit.
64tl Richard III, 72cr siege tower. Bridgeman Art
Library, London: 50tl Canterbury Tales. 70-71
capture of Acre. Biblioteca Estense,
Modena/Bridgeman Art Library: 45br Sungod.
Bibliotheque Nationale Paris/Bridgeman Art
Library: 19br tapestry of stone masons. 51tr Pillage
of Jerusalem. Hedingham Castle/Bridgeman Art
Library, London: 59tl Great hall. Lauros
Girandon/Bridgeman Art Library: 30-31 tapestry,
59br River of Paradise. V & A Museum/Bridgeman
Art Library, London: 32cl, Henry VI at
Westminster. ©British Museum: 13tc, 61tl. The
Danish Tourist Board: Lennard 93cl. ET Archive:
73br. The J. Allan Cash Photolibrary: 17bl, 93br,
96bc, 97br. JNTO: Bill Hobdell 84/85, 106cl.
©Museum of London: 63tl. Loches Castle: 82r. By
courtesy of Luxembourg National Tourist Office:
92tl. Michael Holford: 22tr, 34br, 61bl. National
Guild of Stone Masons: 18bl, 18bfl, 18br, 18bfr,
19tl, 19cl. Robert Harding Picture Library: 83cl,
94tr. Board of Trustees of the Armouries: front
cover cr, 55r, 55bl, 79bc. Sonia Halliday
Photographs: 103b, 103tl, 104bl. Crown
Copyright/ Historic Royal Places: 61tr. Wales
Tourist Board: 25tr. Reproduced by permission of
the Trustees of the Wallace Collection: front cover
cl, 2tr, 2br, 37br, 37bc, 42cl, 42c, 46c, 46/47b, 47r,
47tl, 48tl, 49cr, 49c, 52bl. Weald &
Downland Open Air Museum: back cover tc, 19cr,
64/65b, 65tr, 67tl, 67br. York Archaeological Trust:
63br, 65br. Zefa Pictures: 101tl, 82tl, 92bl, 93tc,
95tl, 95tr, 97tc.